Blueprints

blueprint **1a :** a photographic print in white on a bright blue ground made usu. on paper or cloth . . . and used esp. for copying maps, mechanical drawings, and architects' plans
2: a detailed, thoroughly coordinated plan or program of action for effecting some policy or achieving some goal or solution
3: any pattern of action or statement of views, principles, or rules regarded as a guiding program for the achievement of some large objective or objectives
Webster's Third New International Dictionary

Blueprints

Lloyd Elder

BROADMAN PRESS
Nashville, Tennessee

4265-81
ISBN: 0-8054-6581-2

Dewey Decimal Classification: 286
Subject Heading: SOUTHERN BAPTISTS
Library of Congress Catalog Card Number: 84-7634
Printed in the United States of America

All Scripture quotations are from the *New American Standard Bible.* Copyright © the Lockman Foundation, 1960, 1962, 1968, 1971, 1972, 1973, 1975, 1977. Used by permission.

Library of Congress Cataloging in Publication Data

Elder, Lloyd, 1933-
    Blueprints: 10 challenges for a great people.

    1. Southern Baptist Convention—Doctrines.
2. Baptists—Doctrines. 3. Church renewal—Baptists.
I. Title.
BX6462.7.E43 1984   286′.132   84-7634
ISBN 0-8054-6581-2

To Sue
my companion of more than three decades—
loving, strong, gentle

To special, local Baptist congregations
who have cared for us and
helped mold our ministry

To a host of fellow Baptists
who have touched our lives for good
and challenged us to renewal in the faith

A Personal Introduction

A Great People

Southern Baptists are indeed a great people. At least that is my own personal estimate, and it seems to be shared by literally thousands like me across this land. "A great but not a perfect people" best describes my own experience and knowledge after more than half a century in our denominational family.

Why risk such a claim about Southern Baptists—"a great people"? I have thought about that and am willing to take the risk because I see Southern Baptists as:

- great in their faith in Christ as Lord and Savior, one-by-one;
- great in their dependence on Holy Scripture;
- great in their contribution to the world missionary movement;
- great in their local church polity and cooperation;
- great in their service to God and humanity;
- great in their rich and costly heritage;
- great in their common touch with the masses of people;
- great in their raising up of good and gifted leaders;
- great in heroic stands on issues that matter in the long scope of Christianity;
- great in their spirit and fellowship;
- great in their size, programs, and institutions;
- great in their purpose and potential for continued service to God and humanity;
- yes, and great also in the way they have dealt with me during every turn in my journey.

Southern Baptists—a great people! Forgive me if you think otherwise; if you think it an immodest claim; if you have become disappointed with, or even cynical about us as Southern Baptists. But deep down I am an unapologetic, openminded, probing, committed member of the Southern Baptist family. And just how did I get this way?

Living Among These People

My own journey through the years has been in the midst of these people and has contributed to my deep appreciation for Southern Baptists.

I was born into a Southern Baptist family, the fourteenth of fifteen children—God's gift to Joseph and Dorris Elder—right in the heart of the Great Depression. Really, in 1933 our family did not take note of the "heart" of the depression—it didn't seem to have much of a beginning or ending.

During the 1930s we were a family on the move—and not on a company expense account, either. Like many families we were looking for work, trying to put together an honest living for a large family by the manpower of every family member, including the younger Elders. Dad was a craftsman and a small businessman. He either made or bought wholesale items that we sold retail to homes and small businesses.

By the time I was eight years old, we had traveled through twenty-four states. Before I started to school, I had learned to read from the Burma Shave signs along the highways. In school, I was always the new kid in the class from the big family down the street. At home things were always interesting, forever noisy, and often fun, even if we had to look for it.

During World War II, we settled for awhile in my hometown, Dallas, Texas, where Dad and Mother worked in defense plants. I actually went to the same school and to the same Baptist Sunday School for three years in a row! Then we moved to a small farm in East Texas where I learned to like school, work hard, go barefooted in the sand, and do without things.

Again, during those three years a small Baptist church became a significant part of the Elder family life.

During those childhood years I soaked up many experiences and learned some lessons—not all of them pleasant.

- As children we were loved and cared for, but life revolved mainly around survival, not rights and privileges.
- In that large family, we were often uprooted and forever poor but intensely proud.
- We learned to work hard, but that hard work was not always rewarded.
- The long series of transitional experiences and deprivation must have wounded my spirit, leaving a loss of self-esteem that was with me well into my adult years.
- But whether in boyhood flights of fantasy or in quiet resolve, I lived out those years and dreamed of a better day.
- Older brothers and sisters who had broken out of the family cycle turned back to share their own encouragement and affirmation with the younger set.

High school for me was a countdown to decision. Four years to decide what to do with my life—then three, then only two, and then my senior year. Things had turned around and good experiences were coming my way—at least I thought so: basketball, football, track, honor society, and girls! I knew I ought to do something worthwhile with my life, but what? As a developing young man, I painfully struggled with that question far more than my happy-go-lucky manner allowed me to show.

The summer of 1951, between my junior and senior years in high school, I went with my older brother, Carl, to Fairbanks, Alaska, to "make a lot of money in construction." And I did. But something far better happened. In a rented attic room I knelt beside my bed and received Christ as my Savior and Lord. The following night that confession was made public, and I was baptized into the fellowship of the First Southern Baptist Church, Fairbanks. By whom? By a summer missionary, Robin Guess from

Howard Payne College, a Texas Baptist school. Deep, abiding joy settled in.

Now the struggle about my life's purpose took on a new dimension. My older brother, Carl, felt called to preach. I wasn't about to follow in Carl's steps and become a preacher; yet the thought did keep coming to my mind. However, I decided to go to college and become a history teacher. Mother and I often talked about my sense of direction. She prayed for me but never decided my future.

In the fall of 1952, just before going away to college, my closest friend asked, "Lloyd, don't you think God's calling you to preach?"

"No, I don't, Joe, but if he does, I'll do it!" I retorted, only to be snared by my own words.

In an evening revival service at Field City Baptist Church in Dallas, I made a public commitment to special service! God had called me to preach. With fear and joy and the guidance of my pastor, Bill James Bell, I set about the task and preparation for it.

At Decatur Baptist College, I met Sue Bristow, a Baptist deacon's lovely daughter from Frisco, Texas. In addition to going to school that year, we dated, courted, fell in love, got engaged, and got married in September before our sophomore year.

In the spring of 1956, Sue and I graduated from Howard Payne College and headed for Southwestern Baptist Theological Seminary. That seminary experience turned out to be a decade that grounded me thoroughly in biblical studies, pastoral ministry, and Baptist cooperation.

Southern Baptists have touched our lives together for good during these more than thirty years—twenty-two of them in the ministry of local congregations. I cannot thank our Lord enough for the privilege of pastoring eight Baptist churches. The four student pastorates shaped and challenged Sue and me. I was encouraged by the small seven-member mission at Big Delta, Alaska; and we were loved, trusted, and followed by the Baptist people in three Texas student pastorates: Mount Zion, Pleasant Hill, and Ida Baptist Churches.

The First Baptist Churches of Holland, Texas, and of Princeton, Texas, taught me to love and care and reach out and build and discipline my time and cultivate my gifts. First Baptist Church, College Station, Texas, challenged me to blend serious study, biblical preaching, pastoral care, and church growth and development.

Gambrell Street Baptist Church, Fort Worth, Texas, my last and longest pastoral responsibility, added three additional dimensions to my Southern Baptist experience:

(1) I began to know personally Baptist missionaries and teachers and leaders from across the nation and world. (2) I began to participate in Baptist life not only in the association but also in the state convention and Southern Baptist agencies. (3) My family received ministry in great sorrow, for the Gambrell Street people "pastored" us following an auto accident in 1970 when our eleven-year-old daughter, Janet Lynne, was killed and my wife, Sue, and two other children, Donna Sue, and Philip Lloyd, received serious injuries. Months and years of healing were experienced among those great Baptist people.

The personal journey is not over. I have shared just enough to give the testimony behind my perspective. With all of our troubles, differences, and shortcomings, Southern Baptists are a great people. I count it as one of life's profound joys to be numbered in the family. But why this book? And why now?

Blueprints

Southern Baptists, my denominational family, are moving through some troubled times right now. And I care deeply. Others care too. This book is an effort to say, "I care." It's an effort to say that I believe in our Baptist people and that positive, constructive work can be done.

Blueprints is a book rooted in the following diverse experiences in my own life:

1. Pastoral concern for people nurtured and expressed in

more than two decades in local churches, always with a yearning for spiritual renewal.

2. Participation in the program leadership team of the Baptist General Convention of Texas, a group of people who really care about the churches, the Baptist work, and a large number of lost people.

3. Administrative leadership in Southwestern Baptist Theological Seminary where we tried to allocate our limited resources to specific objectives in theological education.

4. Considerable study and training in how institutions and organizations live and move and have their being, that is, management philosophy and practice, including organization renewal.

5. Involvement in orientation as the new president of the Baptist Sunday School Board, which has brought to me a new sense of denominational heritage, administrative responsibility, worldwide spiritual need, and a dawning, fresh hope for the future.

Blueprints began to emerge first as a concept for Sunday School Board leadership responsibility, then as challenges to our great Baptist people. The thesis of the book is: *as a people of God, let us earnestly seek and work together toward the spiritual and organization renewal of our Southern Baptist denomination.* This thesis has behind it the following assumptions:

• Southern Baptists are a great people, and they are my people. I belong to them, and I care deeply what happens to us. The denomination is troubled on many sides.

• On the one hand, we are a people of God needing spiritual renewal from God in whose hands our destiny lies. On the other hand, we are like a large human organization with a beginning and a potential ending of fragmentation or even death.

• If Southern Baptists know who we are, where we are in the life cycle of the denomination, what it will take to experience spiritual and organization renewal, we can and will rise up by the thousands, if not millions, to act upon our commitment to Christ, to one another, and to a lost world.

• As Southern Baptists, we need renewal throughout the

whole denomination and within every church and Baptist entity. But organization renewal cannot be done *for us*. The hard, constructive work of renewing the denomination is God's work that also belongs to every Baptist who will join his work crew.

• So, like a set of blueprints for building a house, these ten challenges are presented, not to do the work of renewal but to set forth *how it can be done* and done well by a great people.

These times in our denomination are challenging but very hopeful! My effort to bring the principles of organization renewal and management practices together with spiritual renewal and biblical theology has its limitations. I realize that. But I think the effort is valid, and it is my prayer that it will be helpful. Should my effort make even a small contribution as God's people called Southern Baptists build for a better day of service in the kingdom, I shall forever be grateful. But ultimately in all matters pertaining to our denomination, we must always be a people who look for a city whose builder and maker is God. Now *Blueprints: 10 Challenges for a Great People!*

Acknowledgments

This writing project has been my own consuming, personal responsibility but supported in an excellent way by a strong team at the Sunday School Board.

Steve Bond, Broadman editor, has provided not only excellent editorial assistance but has joined me in thinking through the major concepts and has helped to sharpen their presentation. He has been an encouraging, tough-minded colleague.

Gomer Lesch, special assistant to the Executive Office, assisted in research and drafting in the area of communications, change, and conflict. Review of major resources was provided by Howard Gallimore, Sadie Steagald, and Bill Sumners of Dargan-Carver Library and by Larry Yarborough of the Personnel Department.

Sue Elder, my companion of thirty years, reviewed major biblical texts for the concepts involved in each chapter. Even more significantly, she provided needed encouragement and insight throughout the project. Joyce Byrd, secretary to the president, was supportive at every turn along the way, including scheduling discipline.

I would like to thank those who responded to a denominational leadership survey. In doing so, they responded to the following question: *If you could give encouraging counsel to the Southern Baptist family, what would you exhort them to do?*

Each chapter contains some of the responses to this question. My thanks to Lewis Wingo of the Research Services Department for the excellent work he did in helping formulate and interpret the survey.

Contents

1
Denomination Renewal

Challenge #1: As a people of God, let us earnestly seek to work together toward the spiritual and organization renewal of our Southern Baptist denomination by

(1) Understanding the nature of our denomination as a spiritual/human organization;

(2) Analyzing honestly where we are in spiritual development and organizational growth;

(3) Experiencing personal renewal and initiating a renewal process for managing changes toward greater denominational maturity; and

(4) Committing the total resources of the denomination toward a larger contribution in the work of God's kingdom.

Luke 14:27-28: Whoever does not carry his own cross and come after Me cannot be My disciple. For which one of you when he wants to build a tower, does not first sit down and calculate the cost, to see if he has enough to complete it?

Hebrews 3:4-6: For every house is built by someone, but the builder of all things is God. Now Moses was faithful in all His house as a servant, for a testimony of those things which were to be spoken later; but Christ was faithful as a Son over His house whose house we are, if we hold fast our confidence and boast of our hope firm until the end.

Organization Renewal: Organization Renewal is the process of initiating, creating and confronting needed changes so as to make it possible for organizations to become or remain viable, to adapt to new conditions, to solve problems, to learn from experiences, and to move toward greater organizational maturity. . . . Organization Development is the strengthening of those human processes in organizations which improve the functioning of the organic system so as to achieve its objectives.

GORDON L. LIPPITT[1]

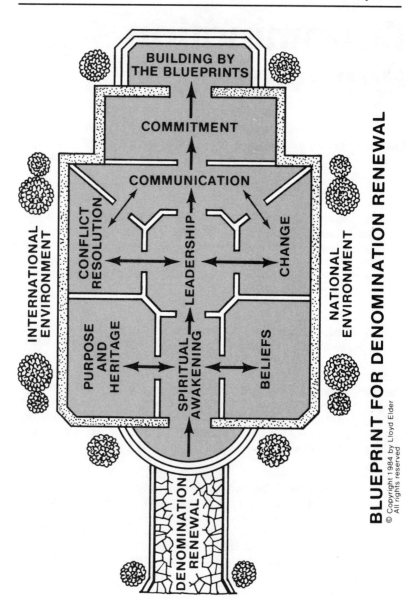

BUILDING BY
THE BLUEPRINTS

COMMITMENT

COMMUNICATION

CONFLICT
RESOLUTION

LEADERSHIP

CHANGE

INTERNATIONAL
ENVIRONMENT

PURPOSE
AND
HERITAGE

SPIRITUAL
AWAKENING

BELIEFS

NATIONAL
ENVIRONMENT

DENOMINATION
RENEWAL

BLUEPRINT FOR DENOMINATION RENEWAL

During the past decade Southern Baptists set an awesome goal. By the year AD 2000 we want to make it possible for every person in the world to have the opportunity to hear and respond to the gospel of Christ.

Just as we began to move toward that goal, tremors were felt in our denomination. Some of our Baptist people believe these tremors are the beginning of a major earthquake that will eventually fragment Southern Baptists into two or more separate bodies.

I am strongly committed to the goals of Bold Mission Thrust. And yet I also hear and feel these tremors. We cannot just cry slogans related to Bold Mission and hope that all will be well. We must understand and attend to the rumble, the disharmony that Southern Baptists are experiencing, if we want to move toward our goals.

I believe in Southern Baptists. This book grows out of that belief and confidence as I offer *Blueprints: 10 Challenges for a Great People.*

One of the strong convictions that underlies this book is that how we see our situation is very important. What we do about it will largely be determined by how we perceive what's happening to us.

What is the meaning of the noises among us? Many believe that the noise would stop if those who disagreed with them would just get out of the denomination. If that happened, who would be left? Have you ever known two Baptists who agree with each other on everything?

Others see the disharmony as the work of the devil in opposition to the Bold Mission Thrust effort. No doubt some of it is. But I believe much of it is something else as well. I believe our denomination is in the midst of growing pains. As we are caught up in such a crisis, the tempter will work overtime to try to keep us from going on to a new level of maturity and reaching our Bold Mission Thrust goals.

In this chapter, I will compare our situation with the life cycles of plants, animals, persons, and especially organizations. Seeing ourselves as a people of God in a time of transition from one level of maturity to another throws a lot of light on what we're experiencing. More important, it suggests some constructive actions we can take to cooperate with the growth and maturity we're being called to as a people of God.

I am seeking to join you and other Southern Baptists in understanding where we are as a people of God and working for the renewal of our denomination. The indispensable foundation of denomination renewal is spiritual renewal in the lives of individual Southern Baptists. We can understand the principles and practice of organization renewal, we can take action and initiatives within the denomination with a view toward renewal, but unless there is a group of people who are daily being renewed by the Spirit of God, all our efforts will be empty and in vain. I pray that we will experience the quickening, life-giving outpouring of God's Spirit in discerning and being willing to follow God's will in his kingdom's work and in our relationships with each other. The fruit of such renewal will be a commitment of our total resources—human, financial, physical, and spiritual—toward:

(1) Remaining true to our spiritual nature as a people of God;
(2) Maintaining our democratic and voluntary relationships;
(3) Fulfilling our worldwide missionary-evangelistic purpose; and
(4) Being God's people and channels of his grace to a sad, broken world.

The Stages of Life

All life as we know it grows in stages. This is true of both plants and animals. One of the most striking examples of this is the butterfly. An egg comes first, then a caterpillar. The caterpillar weaves a cocoon, and for a time it appears there is no life at all. Then the cocoon bursts, and from it flies a magnificent butterfly. Human life occurs in stages too. Paul recognized this when he said, "When I was a child, I used to speak as a child, . . . when I became a man, I did away with childish things" (1 Cor. 13:11).

Those who have studied organizations have borrowed this picture of life cycles found in plants, animals, and persons. This picture helps them to better understand and explain what happens in human organizations. They have found this picture particularly helpful in understanding crisis times in organizations.

These students of organizations have pointed out that such crisis times are like transition times in the development of a butterfly. Or, they are like adolescence or mid-life crises in human life. An organizational crisis is neither good nor bad. It just is. In every crisis, there is both vulnerability and opportunity. There is potential for regression and disintegration, as well as opportunity for growth and greater maturity.

In this chapter, I would like to suggest that we as Southern Baptists are now in a transition phase of our life cycle as a people of God. Seeing where we are and realizing what's happening among us can reduce the level of fear. This will help us clarify our options and allow the crisis to strengthen our denomination rather than break it apart.

Southern Baptists—An Overview

Before reviewing what is happening in the Southern Baptist denomination, it would be helpful to understand who and what we are. The Southern Baptist denomination is a designation given to an extensive organic network of Christian believers in local churches and related organizations who:

- Bear a common name;
- Share a mutual heritage;
- Confess distinctive beliefs;
- Practice a democratic/congregational polity;
- Experience a unity of consciousness;
- Enjoy a corporate fellowship;
- Cooperate through associations, state conventions, and a na-

tional convention called the Southern Baptist Convention;
• Elicit, combine, and direct their energies for the one sacred effort of propagating the gospel; and
• Implement a comprehensive, worldwide Christian missionary enterprise.

As you can see from Figure 1-1, the Southern Baptist denomination as it exists today is an amazing network of individuals, churches, and organizations that voluntarily cooperate together in a corporate fellowship to perform a common task. (See also the Southern Baptist Time Line, inside front cover.)

The Southern Baptist denomination is a creation of self-governing, New Testament churches. Associations exist only by the voluntary consent of the local churches. So it is with state Baptist conventions and the Southern Baptist Convention.

The denominational structures created by local churches continually owe their existence to the voluntary consent and support of local churches. Once denominational structures are created, they have considerable influence on the local church. But again, this influence occurs only with the consent of local churches. And at all times denominational structures of all kinds are accountable to the churches and to trustees who are elected by state conventions or the Southern Baptist Convention. They exist for no other reason than to enable the churches to do cooperatively in missions, education, and benevolent ministries what they could not do alone.

The Southern Baptist denomination is a complex entity made up of a large number of different organizations. It is not a single corporate structure. Rather, it is a network of individuals, churches, and organizations created by the churches to enable them to work together.

I would not for a moment suggest that Southern Baptists are little more than one vast bureaucratic organization. It has been my experience and somewhat knowledgeable assessment that the voluntary network of our 36,000 autonomous churches and related Baptist bodies is, in fact, one of the great strengths of our

Figure 1-1

DENOMINATIONAL CONCEPT:
THE SOUTHERN BAPTIST FAMILY

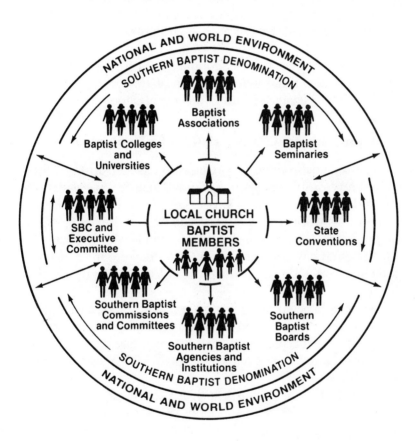

denomination. We work together freely and responsibly because we realize this can help us accomplish tasks we couldn't accomplish independently.

It is true enough that our growing successes have created the need for structures and processes that may be confusing, inconvenient, and at times inefficient. At the same time, these processes have provided a healthy decentralization, a check-and-balance of power and control.

While the Southern Baptist denomination isn't one vast organization with human authority vested in a single person or group, it has many other characteristics of an organization.

Organizational Characteristics of a Denomination

Social scientists define an organization as a structure or network of relationships or groups of individuals in a particular setting and environment with processes by which the structure carries on its work. *Structure* is a static view of the organization, and *process* is a dynamic view. Organization is what is created by human beings who want to concentrate their resources on common endeavors and to carry out those tasks as efficiently as possible.

Once people begin working together and creating an organization that makes cooperation possible, the organization grows in complexity. It experiences a life cycle much like plants and animals. An organization begins with birth and goes through a number of stages.

The work of social scientists, such as Gordon Lippitt, who have studied the life cycles of organizations may throw helpful light on what we Southern Baptists are currently experiencing. Of course, from a theological viewpoint, we believe that the Southern Baptist denomination was born within the purposes of God. But after recognizing that, it is still illuminating to study the stages that human organizations go through and to apply those insights to Southern Baptists today. Seeing what's happening in the larger context can bring one the wisdom to make constructive choices in the midst of crisis.

Lippitt sets forth three developmental stages of organizational growth: birth, youth, and maturity. Two critical concerns are dealt with at each stage (see Table 1-1 on next page). In addition to identifying a key issue associated with each critical concern, Lippitt points to what can happen when these concerns are resolved correctly or incorrectly (see Table 1-2).

Lippitt's analysis of the stages of organization development grew out of his study of business organizations. For that reason, some of his terminology cannot easily be applied to the stages of development of the Southern Baptist denomination. Having made this disclaimer, I find much of Lippitt's framework enlightening as a preliminary understanding of our denominational life. I will leave it to historians and students of organization development to examine in some detail how applicable Lippitt's framework is to the development of the Southern Baptist denomination.

Of course, there are other ways of characterizing the life cycle of an organization. Another approach is that of James J. Cribbin found in Table 1-3.

Developmental Stages of the Denomination

I. Birth

 1. Creation and Beginnings

In 1845 a new organizational system called the Southern Baptist Convention came into being. The reasons for the creation of the Southern Baptist Convention are many and complex. Certainly no competent student of history would now deny that slavery and a host of social, economic, and political issues related to slavery influenced the growing desire of Baptists in the South to create their own convention.

But a basic reason for the creation of a denomination of Baptists in the South was their desire to have a means for supporting missions, education, and benevolent work.

TABLE 1-1
Stages of Organizational Growth

Developmental stage	Critical concern	Key issue	Consequences if concern is not met
BIRTH	1. To create a new organization	What to risk	Frustration and inaction
	2. To survive as a viable system	What to sacrifice	Death of organization
			Further subsidy by "faith" capital
YOUTH	3. To gain stability	How to organize	Reactive, crisis-dominated organization
			Opportunistic rather than self-directing attitudes and policies
	4. To gain reputation and develop pride	How to review and evaluate	Difficulty in attracting good personnel and clients
			Inappropriate, overly aggressive, and distorted image building
MATURITY	5. To achieve uniqueness and adaptability	Whether and how to change	Unnecessarily defensive or competitive attitudes; diffusion of energy
			Loss of most creative personnel
	6. To contribute to society	Whether and how to share	Possible lack of public respect and appreciation
			Bankruptcy or profit loss

SOURCE: Gordon L. Lippitt and Warren H. Schmidt, "Crises in a Developing Organization," *Harvard Business Review,* Vol. 45, No. 6, November–December, 1967, p. 103. Copyright © 1967 by the President and Fellows of Harvard College.

TABLE 1-2
Results of Handling Organizational Crises

Critical issue	Result if the issue is resolved . . .	
	Correctly	Incorrectly
CREATION	New organizational system comes into being and begins operating	Idea remains abstract. The organization is undercapitalized and cannot adequately develop and expose product or service
SURVIVAL	Organization accepts realities, learns from experience, becomes viable	Organization fails to adjust to realities of its environment and either dies or remains marginal—demanding continuing sacrifice
STABILITY	Organization develops efficiency and strength, but retains flexibility to change	Organization overextends itself and returns to survival stage, or establishes stabilizing patterns which block future flexibility
PRIDE AND REPUTATION	Organization's reputation reinforces efforts to improve quality of goods and service	Organization places more effort on image-creation than on quality product, or it builds an image which misrepresents its true capability
UNIQUENESS AND ADAPTABILITY	Organization changes to take fuller advantage of its unique capability and provides growth opportunities for its personnel	Organization develops too narrow a specialty to ensure secure future, fails to discover its uniqueness and spreads its efforts into inappropriate areas, or develops a paternalistic stance which inhibits growth
CONTRIBUTION	Organization gains public respect and appreciation for itself as an institution contributing to society.	Organization may be accused of having lost all care for the public interest; or accused of using stockholder funds irresponsibly

SOURCE: Gordon L. Lippitt and Warren H. Schmidt, "Crises in a Developing Organization," *Harvard Business Review,* Vol. 45, No. 6, November–December, 1967, p. 109. Copyright © 1967 by the President and Fellows of Harvard College.

TABLE 1-3. Life cycle of an organization.

Life Stage	Birth	Childhood	Adolescence	Early Maturity	Vigorous Maturity	Ripe Maturity	Senescence	Renewal
Primary objective	Survival	Short-term profit	Accelerated growth	Systematic growth	Balanced growth	Uniqueness, image	Maintenance	Revitalization
Leader type	Innovator	Opportunist	Consultant	Participant	Corporateur	Statesman	Administrator	Mover and shaker
Organizational character	Struggling	Achieving	Changing	Expanding, diversifying	Systems-oriented	Mature, self-satisfied	Status quo–oriented	Change-oriented
Organizational self-image	Self-centered	Local	Sectional	National	Multinational	Cosmopolitan	Complacent	Self-critical
Energy focus	The new and novel	Competing	Conquering	Coordinating	Integrating, controlling	Adjusting	Continuing existence	Renewing, developing
Central problem	Market entry	Existence	Market share	Multifaceted growth	Centralization and autonomy	Balancing divergent interests	Stability	Rejuvenation
Type of planning	Visionary	Catch-as-catch-can	Simple: sales, budgets	Formal: orderly, specialized	Sophisticated: a way of life	Social, political	Extrapolative	Creative
Management mode	One person	Small in-group	Delegated	Decentralized	Centralized	Collegial	Tradition-bound	Striving, driving
Organizational model	Maximization of profit	Optimization of profit	Planned profit	Good citizenship	Social responsibility	Social institution	Bureaucracy	Imitation of the Phoenix

Reprinted, by permission of the publisher, from LEADERSHIP: STRATEGIES FOR ORGANIZATIONAL EFFECTIVENESS by James J. Cribbin, p. 49 © 1981 by AMACOM, a division of American Management Associations, New York. All rights reserved.

Poor communication between Baptists of the North and South also had a lot to do with their growing apart. Baptists in the South, perhaps without cause, felt that the American Baptist Home Mission Society was neglecting the South as an area of mission work. The sectionalism that had existed from colonial days was deeply rooted and was surely an important factor that caused Baptists in the South to form their own organization.

2. Survival and Expansion

The Southern Baptist Convention wasn't born with a silver spoon in its mouth. In the first fifteen to twenty years of its existence, it faced a number of issues that could well have been its undoing.

The major task it faced was enlisting Baptist churches in the South in a missions effort both at home and overseas. The problems of transportation and communication in 1845 were enough to threaten and frustrate the new Convention.

Another key problem the new Convention faced was the strong Calvinistic theology that dominated the South. Calvinistic theology, when pressed to the extreme, is antimissionary.

The prevailing view of church government in the area west of the Appalachian Mountains emphasized the local church so strongly that cooperation among local churches was feared as a possible threat to New Testament polity.

If these difficulties and obstacles weren't enough, only fifteen years after its beginning, the young Convention faced the horror of the Civil War. The war and the years of Reconstruction that followed became a severe test of the denomination's will to exist. During the years of Reconstruction, suggestions were made from time to time that the denomination reunite with Northern Baptists. By 1879 it was evident that the denomination would survive. At the Southern Baptist Convention of 1879 a resolution was adopted which expressed a willingness to cooperate with Northern Baptists but which communicated the desire to remain separate from them as an organization.

II. Youth

   3. Stability and Identity

In 1891 Southern Baptists established themselves in the fields of publishing and educational services. This was an important step in the growth and maturation of the denomination. Earlier attempts had been made to enter the publishing field, but each of these had failed. By 1891 Southern Baptists were ready for the next step. Although there was resistance to this step on the part of influential leaders, the success of the new venture was not long in coming. The Sunday School Board, with its publishing and educational programs, gave the denomination a growing sense of unity and identity.

In 1888 women's work was formally organized among Southern Baptists. This strengthened the missionary, educational, and benevolent purposes of the denomination. It also gave Southern Baptists a sense of unity as a corporate body.

   4. Pride and Reputation

As a growing organization, the denomination sought to improve its methods of support and services by establishing the Cooperative Program in 1925. A host of new beginnings in Southern Baptist life were taking place at this stage of the denomination's life. These developments brought the denomination to the forefront among all non-Catholic Christian denominations in both the nation and the world (see Southern Baptist Time Line).

III. Maturity

   5. Uniqueness and Change

It is my opinion that, during the fourteen decades of its life, the Southern Baptist Convention has come through the stages of birth, childhood, and youth and is entering the stage of maturity. If this is so, it might be well for us to review Gordon Lippitt's concept of organizational maturity. According to Lippitt, there are two crises of maturity in an organization. In the first crisis, the critical concern is to achieve uniqueness and adaptability. The key issue is whether and how to change.

If the critical concern is not met, defensive and competitive attitudes prevail, and energy is diffused. If the critical concern is met but the issue is resolved incorrectly, according to Lippitt, "the organization develops too narrow a specialty to ensure secure future, fails to discover its uniqueness, and spreads its efforts into inappropriate areas, or develops a paternalistic stance which inhibits growth."[2]

On the other hand, if the issue is resolved correctly, "the organization changes to take fuller advantage of its unique capability and provides growth opportunities for its personnel" (Lippitt's business orientation).

As I look at our great denomination and try to measure it honestly in the light of its long history, I must admit that we are passing through troubled times. The controversy is often described as one of beliefs—primarily beliefs concerning the nature of the Bible.

While this is certainly a part of the controversy, it is not the core issue. *I believe ours is primarily a crisis of change.* We have been enormously successful as a denomination. Success brings with it certain changes. The test of a growing, successful organization is whether it can make the organizational changes necessary to operate with the successes it has achieved. Whether and how Southern Baptists are willing to change may test our maturity and determine to what extent we will be prepared for usefulness to God and for our next stage of development. In a later chapter, I deal with change and the changeless dimension of our Baptist fellowship.

6. Contribution and Creativity

If renewal does take place in the life of our people and among our leaders, churches, conventions, agencies, and institutions, we would then be ready to make our greatest contribution in the world. We would likely gain widespread public respect and more importantly the accolade of our Lord, "Well done."

But if there is no renewal at this critical fifth stage (see Table

1-1) in our denominational journey, then we may not be able to continue business as usual, let alone reach our bold dream for AD 2000.

Symptoms of Crisis

I have suggested that we are in a crisis of change in our denomination. Following are some of the specific symptoms I see that support my belief:

- A growing need to operate routinely and within policies and program assignments rather than seeing policy and purpose in the light of goals;
- Reluctance to face hard facts and truths about ourselves;
- Fearful resistance to change;
- Oversimplifying the issues and answers related to the denomination;
- Fearing the consequences of rocking the denominational boat;
- Trap of either institutional or individualistic thinking and values;
- Heavy dependence on past patterns, methodologies, and successes;
- Diffusion of denominational purposes and objectives;
- Lack of a denominational decision-making system;
- Inadequate relationship between the denomination and its external environment and needs; and
- Commitment to one's own personal goals above the goals of Christ's kingdom.

While I am deeply aware of the greatness of our people and of our potential for greater service to God and others, I am not blind to our present needs, concerns, and differences. A lifetime of living within this fellowship and years of working, relating, reading, and listening have opened my eyes to the needs for renewal within the denomination.

Theologians and sociologists have written of our age as a postdenominational era. Persons of widely differing theological stances have claimed that denominations are no longer useful or vital to the work of the church. I don't believe it! But I do believe that we must listen to one another about the perceived ills within the denominational body.

Without elaboration, let me summarize a diversity of opinion being printed in the press, spoken from platforms, and talked about in conference rooms and coffee shops where Southern Baptists meet:

1. Liberalism, some say, is creeping into the denomination—especially into the schools and the Sunday School Board.
2. Fundamentalism of the divisive, creedal type is seeking to take over the power structures of the denomination, according to others.
3. A power struggle, according to yet another opinion, is being waged between those who have been giving leadership to the denomination and those who have been most prominent in leading influential churches.
4. Others believe there is an erosion of confidence in the nature and authority of the Bible evidenced by the refusal of some to believe in "the inerrancy of Scripture."
5. There is a questioning of basic Baptist beliefs even by some in our institutions commissioned to uphold our doctrines and values, some Southern Baptists believe.
6. Others point to a need for spiritual awakening among members of the churches—awakening toward vital Christian faith and discipleship in the local churches.
7. There is a loss of zeal and enthusiasm in evangelism—in reaching the lost with the saving gospel of Christ—some people charge.
8. Others cry that there is an emergence of secular humanism in American society that is supported by some Southern Baptists in the name of separation of church and state.
9. Others believe that Southern Baptists have lost their sense of mission, that they are drifting from their founding purpose.
10. Southern Baptists have forgotten or neglected their heritage,

some people are saying. This means we have come to an identity crisis of major proportions.

11. Southern Baptists are an aging denomination with aging agencies and institutions, according to others. We are suffering from the winding down of spiritual energy and increasing weight of layers of institutionalism.

12. Still another often-voiced opinion is that Southern Baptists are becoming bigger and even more diverse with expansion in land mass, enlargement in numbers, and extension into new segments and layers of society.

13. Some believe that Southern Baptists face a major leadership crisis—too much supply of able and gifted leadership in the old South and too few leaders willing to serve in the challenging pioneer areas of our nation and world.

14. Others among us believe that Southern Baptists have limited resources to do the work they know to do—at least as those resources are now distributed primarily in the local churches.

15. Another opinion often heard is that communication among Southern Baptists is not adequate, consistent, or trustworthy.

16. Southern Baptists are slowly losing spiritual momentum as they are on the threshold of increased usefulness, some people charge.

17. According to others, Southern Baptists are still too private in their faith, not regarding the concerns and needs of humanity around the world, including hunger, population, war, and human rights.

18. Other voices in the debate admit that Southern Baptists have always had problems. We have periodically faced crisis. Let us now learn what we can from one another, resolve the issues, and get on with the work God has given us to do.

Denomination Renewal—An Overview

These various diagnoses show that Southern Baptists are not in agreement on the key problems of the denomination. That in

Encouraging counsel to the Southern Baptist family:

As Southern Baptists, we should remember that we walk together in faith under God's leadership. It is easy to recognize that we are a diverse group and, therefore, our love and understanding should bind us together in a Christian fellowship. Together we strive to achieve the Great Commission. Our greatest commitment is our personal loyalty to Jesus Christ, and our witness in the world reflects on him for good or ill.

Harold C. Bennett, Exec. Sec.-Treas., Executive Committee, SBC

Do not forget we are essentially a grass-roots people. Magnify the Lord Jesus in all our plans and programs. Let us return to a deeper spiritual life in prayer and consecration!

J. D. Grey, President, SBC, 1952-1955

Magnify the quality of personal relationship with Jesus Christ as the dynamic power for individual discipleship and our corporate participation in God's mission in his world.

Roy L. Honeycutt, President, Southern Seminary

We have sought to "stir up the gift of God within": finding unswerving confidence in the Bible as God's Word, genuine trust of each other as believers, and growing confidence in our work together through the churches for evangelism, missions, education, and benevolence.

W. Randall Lolley, President, Southeastern Seminary

With all my heart, I believe that Southern Baptists must rediscover and reaffirm that our mission is both evangelism and education, word and deed, witness and works, conversion and character, proclamation and practice. Both are essential if we are to carry out the Commission our Lord gave us.

Harry Piland, Dir., Sunday School Department, BSSB

Our most important task is seeing the lostness of our beloved nation and being concerned enough to make evangelism (witnessing to the lost) an authentic and valid priority.

William G. Tanner, President, Home Mission Board, SBC

itself seems to add fuel to the conflict. But it doesn't have to. Our appraisals of where we are as a denomination will differ. We need to hear each other with a willingness to acknowledge truth regardless of who utters it.

In this chapter, I have suggested where I think we are as a denomination. I believe we are in a time of developmental crisis as an organization. We are in need of renewal—of conscious, intentional intervention. I have drawn on the insights of Gordon Lippitt whose work with business organizations led him to see six stages in the life cycle of such organizations. At the crisis point Lippitt finds that renewal is essential if the organization is to move on to the next stage of its life cycle.

Lippitt defines organization renewal as "the process of initiating, creating, and confronting needed changes so as to make it possible for organizations to become or remain viable, to adapt to new conditions, to solve problems, to learn from experiences, and to move toward greater organizational maturity."[3]

As we regard our denomination as an organization, there is a wealth of information available to us in the field of organization development and renewal. The basic issues and elements most often dealt with can be expressed in the following questions:

- What is the nature and purpose of the denomination to be changed or renewed?
- What are its basic objectives and goals and how are they established?
- What are the needs and problems calling for renewal?
- What are the central beliefs, values, and norms of the denomination?
- How can the denomination react appropriately to the internal and external influences affecting its very being?
- Does the denomination have an effective decision-making process? How are such decisions implemented throughout the denomination?
- What is the ability of denominational leadership to cope with change?

- How is resistance to change dealt with?
- How can the denomination solve problems and resolve conflicts?
- What is the formal and informal communication process? Is it an effective network that is open and clear?
- Does the environment of the denomination encourage and channel creativity by people throughout the denomination?
- Is there a maturity of individuals and groups throughout the denomination, as well as among its leadership?
- Is there a commitment on the part of the denomination to its people and of all its people to the denomination?
- Is there a vitality level in the denomination and its subunits that provides an energetic driving force for the total denomination?

I offer this book as a blueprint for denomination renewal. I don't think of it as a final and finished blueprint. But I do deal with issues and concerns in the rest of the book that I think any plan for renewal within the denomination will have to grapple with.

Although the language of organization development and renewal as secular concerns doesn't sound like the language of Zion, renewal of secular organizations depends on a high level of moral if not spiritual development. Organization renewal calls for a desire for truth and understanding—an honesty that can at times be painful. Even in a secular setting, it calls for a change of mind and a willingness to change that we Baptists call *repentance*. Without this, there can be no renewal.

On the back panel of the book jacket and at the beginning of each chapter is a diagram which gives a visual representation of the plan of the book and how the parts relate to each other and contribute to the whole.

At the center of the diagram is *leadership*. Leadership is at the heart of the renewal process. Leadership is where the work of God's Spirit within is translated into action in the world. I speak of those in positions of leadership but far more. If our Baptist ideals were realized, each Christian would be a leader in the sense of being responsive and obedient to God's leadership in his life and so in the life of the church.

The subject of leadership is so important to the renewal process that I have given a great deal of attention to it in chapter 5. I begin chapter 5 by giving an overview of the centers of authority and influence within our denomination. In addition to this, I enumerate the various leadership roles we have in the denomination. Seeing the large number of leadership roles and centers of authority is an important first step in working for renewal within the denomination.

I then move to consider several different leadership styles. I address the question, What kind of leaders are needed for being agents of renewal in the Southern Baptist denomination?

Chapters 2, 3, and 4 deal with spiritual conditions of renewal. Chapter 2 shows the vital relationship between appropriating our Baptist heritage and being a people prepared to carry out God's purposes. Chapter 3 deals with the vital role of beliefs and doctrine among Southern Baptists. Chapter 4 is a call to personal spiritual awakening.

Genuine spiritual renewal is expressed in action. It is expressed in dealing with real issues of communication (ch. 6), change (ch. 7), and conflict (ch. 8). These three matters are interrelated and as such provide immense potential for productive, creative denominational action.

Chapter 9 calls for a commitment to action. Here I have sketched a dream of what might happen if we Southern Baptists should experience renewal. In chapter 10, the challenge is presented to build upon Jesus Christ, the solid Rock, in the years ahead.

Notes

1. Gordon L. Lippitt, *Organization Renewal* (New York: Meredith Corporation, 1969), pp. 1-2. Throughout this book, I use *denomination renewal* to parallel Lippitt's use of *organization renewal*.

2. Ibid., p. 1.

3. Ibid., p. 2.

2
Purpose and Heritage

Challenge #2: As a people of God, let us recover our central purpose and rediscover the richness of our heritage so that we establish our sense of identity, strengthen the bonds of our unity, and go on to make significant contributions in the sacred work of the gospel of Christ.

Psalm 16:5-6: The Lord is the portion of my inheritance and my cup; thou dost support my lot. The lines have fallen to me in pleasant places; indeed, my heritage is beautiful to me.

Ephesians 3:20-21: Now to Him who is able to do exceeding abundantly beyond all that we ask or think, according to the power that works within us, to Him be the glory in the church and in Christ Jesus to all generations forever and ever. Amen.

Purpose: Understanding an institution's purpose has always been important, and it will be even more so in the days ahead. It is difficult, if not impossible, to establish sound strategies for creating a new identity for an institution if its current identity is not understood. Planned change requires clear understanding and acceptance of one's current status. Acquiring a better understanding of the institution's mission is a vital first step in resolving many of the issues and difficulties confronting an institution.

J. KENT CARATHERS AND GARY B. LOTT[1]

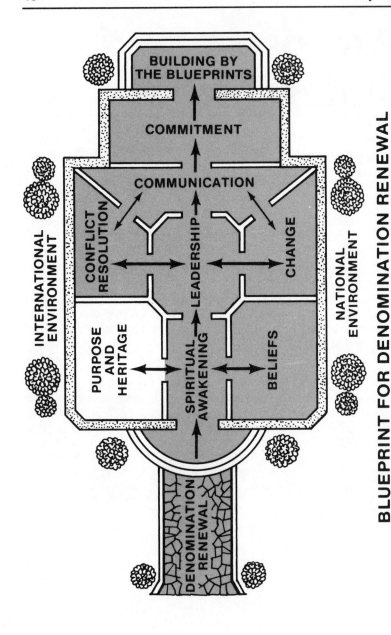

BLUEPRINT FOR DENOMINATION RENEWAL

What have we as Southern Baptists received? What are we doing about it? Where are we going? These are questions I would like to deal with on both a denominational and personal level as we think about renewal in our denomination.

I grew up on a small farm in East Texas. My dad was like many of the farmers in that era who believed that a farmer could be judged by the straightness of the furrows he plowed and the fence rows he built. A crooked fence or furrow was considered a disgrace.

I can remember as if it were yesterday building fences "Dad's way"! On one occasion we began by setting the first corner post strong and true, precisely on the property line. The other corner post was carefully set and well braced. Then Dad backed away and sighted down the line from corner post to corner post. With the posthole diggers, we carefully marked each hole to set the line posts straight between the corner posts.

With that completed, Dad went to other chores leaving my brothers and me to build the fence. One by one we dug the postholes, firmly tamped in the posts, dirt, rocks, and all. Right where Dad had said, directly between the corner posts. Well, almost!

How could Dad have known that one hole would be marked over a large rock, another into the edge of a root, still another near an ant bed? What difference is a three-inch move to the right or six-inch move to the left?

When Dad came back, he went back to the original corner posts. With his keen eye, he looked down the row of posts to the corner post at the other end. "What have you boys done!?" We looked for ourselves. What we saw was a row of posts that no respectable farmer would claim. We had simply made one decision at a time without regard to the corner posts. We had taken the path of expediency.

In our decisions as Southern Baptists, are we not often tempted to take the path of expediency? We make decisions without giving due regard to the insights of those who have gone before us and without considering the consequences for our children.

In a sense our heritage and purpose are like the landmarks of our spiritual possession, our identity as Southern Baptists. In the present chapter I would like to call us to consider these corner posts: our heritage and our purpose.

The Relationship of Heritage to Purpose

Heritage and purpose are related in important ways. Heritage is what we have received. Purpose is what we are doing with what we have received—where we're going with it. Looking at heritage is looking at our past. Purpose is our orientation toward the future, our reason for being.

Consider the relationship between heritage and purpose on the personal level. Mrs. Rogers is a widow. She has two children in high school. Mrs. Rogers has a life insurance policy which ensures that both of her children will have opportunities for training in some vocation or will be able to attend college in the event of her death. If Mrs. Rogers dies, her children will have to recognize the meaning of the papers that constitute Mrs. Rogers's insurance policy. If they don't recognize the meaning of these papers, they could begin adult life with far fewer resources than their mother intended. Their purposes in life will be greatly diminished if they don't understand and appropriate their inheritance. If they know what their inheritance is, their horizons will be greater than if they remained ignorant of their inheritance.

As it is in the case of this family, so it is with us as Southern Baptists. Our heritage and purpose are intimately related. If we are to achieve the purposes God desires for us, we must know who we are—what we have received. If we fail to understand what has been passed on to us, we will have a diminished sense of our purpose.

Over twenty years ago, Dr. Norman Cox, Baptist pastor and historian, wrote in *We Southern Baptists,* "We have had two generations to come and go in our churches with less and less awareness of the chasms that separate us from other denominations in our views of faith." That was over twenty years ago! Not knowing what we have received, we are not able to appropriate those elements in our heritage which would give us a unity in our differences and enable us to see purposes that we can whole-heartedly work toward.

Heritage and Purpose in the New Testament

A Christian is first and foremost someone who has received something. We often think of Christians as people who are givers. And that is right. But giving is secondary for the Christian. Giving is an effect.

To see this in a clear way, consider the apostle Peter. Peter was a man of great natural self-confidence. He was quick to speak and slow to listen. He was bold in trying to defend his Lord against those who came to arrest him. But in a moment of testing, Peter found himself denying the Lord he loved so much. Guilt and bitter remorse engulfed him.

Jesus was taken, tried, and put to death. Being human ourselves, we can well imagine the torment Peter went through between Good Friday and Easter. At such times, we blame ourselves with many rounds of, "If I had only done this rather than that."

Through these trying experiences, Peter learned beyond any doubt that he was spiritually bankrupt. But at the darkest hour, the light broke through. In the hour of greatest need, the gift came. Christ arose. Peter received the forgiving love of his Lord; as he received that gift, Peter's awful deed was transfigured by grace.

On the other side of Jesus' death and resurrection, Peter still didn't have all the answers. He would still make mistakes, but he was a transformed man. In spite of his sin, he was forgiven. As this sense of what he had received grew in him, his sense of purpose grew in scope and strength.

After Peter and John were arrested and brought before the religious leaders in Jerusalem, the leaders warned the two apostles to stop speaking and teaching in the name of Jesus. Peter and John could have focused on their personal safety and security needs and said, "Well, we've done what we could. It may not be healthy to continue this." But no. This is what they said: "Whether it is right in the sight of God to give heed to you rather than to God, you be the judge; for we cannot stop speaking of what we have seen and heard" (Acts 4:19-20). *We cannot stop speaking!*

This is the very heart of where receiving our heritage as Southern Baptists flows into our sense of purpose. Our great need in this day is for us—person by person, church by church, association by association, convention by convention, institution by institution—to be gripped by the gift of God's redemption in Christ in the way that Peter and John were. We need to see, hear, and do; and this will cause us to go, speak, and give to others.

The Distortion of Heritage and Purpose

If the church had stayed at the apostles' level of understanding and motivation, the history of Western civilization and perhaps even world civilization would have been different. But it wasn't to be.

Initially, Christians were in the minority. Collectively they had little or no social, economic, or political power. The only power was the power of the good news energized in the hearts of the listeners by the Holy Spirit.

Not only did Christians not have social approval but they were also aggressively hated and persecuted by the Romans. The rapid spread of Christianity throughout the Roman Empire intensified the persecutions. Historians of the church count at least ten waves of persecution which the church faced from AD 64 to AD 313.

In 313 Constantine and Licinius issued the Edict of Milan which granted freedom to all religions within the Roman Empire. This was what Christians had been longing for—not because they believed that all religions were equally good but because they believed that Christianity was the true faith. They believed they could demand absolute allegiance to Christ only in an environment of religious liberty.

The religious liberty granted by the Edict of Milan was short-lived. The undoing of religious liberty came not in the Roman Empire's opposition to Christianity but in the preferential treatment the emperor soon gave the church.

Constantine saw in Christianity a force that would provide stability, unity, and peace within the Empire. He felt that whatever was good for the church was good for the Empire. For this reason, Constantine intervened in church conflicts for what he felt was the good of the church. Soul freedom as an integral part of Christian faith was nipped in the bud and didn't come to full flower until well after the Reformation.

The alliance of church and state created an environment that resulted in forceful ways of dealing with heretics inside the church and unbelievers outside.

Even with the coming of the Reformation, religious liberty did not flower. Luther defended the right of conscience but approved the death penalty for religious radicals, citing public order as the reason.

In Switzerland, Ulrich Zwingli persecuted radical Protestants led by Conrad Grebel and Felix Manz because further association with them might have endangered his alliance with civil authorities. Zwingli believed that his alliance with civil authorities was important to the well-being of the church. Zwingli approved of Conrad Grebel's death by drowning in Lake Zurich.

In Geneva, John Calvin showed little tolerance toward those who disagreed with him on doctrines, such as predestination and the Trinity. In 1553 Calvin served as a prosecutor for a Spanish heretic, Michael Servetus, who had fled to Geneva after being convicted of heresy in Vienna. Servetus was convicted and burned at the stake October 27, 1553.

The story of intolerance and persecution in religious matters is a long and painful one, hardly touched upon here. It is the story we Southern Baptists need to know. We are what we are because our forefathers believed that persecution, even in the name and for the sake of Christ, is wrong.

Most of us have grown up in a world where religious liberty was and is a given—a gift. Like so many gifts, we have taken it for granted. But we must not. We live in a world where religious liberty is extremely precious. There are forces in every generation that work against it.

In our own generation, the danger is not so much that *we* will be persecuted, although that is a possibility. The greatest danger may be that we will become the persecutors, even within our own denominational family.

We Baptists began as dissenters from a religion that was aligned with civil government. Our Baptist forefathers suffered in English jails, in the Massachusetts Bay Colony, and in Virginia for the right of individuals to believe in God and to live out those beliefs according to conscience.

Now we are the establishment. We are the largest non-Catholic denomination in the United States. We Southern Baptists are "in"—socially, economically, and politically (at least in many quarters). We dare not forget where we have come from. We dare not forget the price that has been paid that we might deal directly with God through his revelation in Christ. We dare not claim for ourselves what we will not grant to others.

You ask, *But aren't we a missionary people? Don't we have a mandate from our Lord to make disciples of all nations?*

Yes. Let there be no misunderstanding about that! The question is one of both theology and methodology. In the next chapter, I will deal with the apparent tension between our desire for true belief and our belief in soul freedom. In what follows, I would like to look at how the Baptist distinctives of soul freedom and missionary purpose are not opposed to each other but, when rightly understood, give strong support to each other.

Jesus, Soul Freedom, and Missionary Purpose

At this point I think it would be helpful to look at Jesus' way of evangelism. You can search the Gospels thoroughly and not find an instance of Jesus trying to force someone into the kingdom of God.

Jesus recognized that the kingdom of God doesn't operate like the kingdoms of this world. He recognized that the response to God's grace was within individuals. It cannot be coerced.

In each of Jesus' three temptations, the devil tried to get Jesus to use nonkingdom means to achieve kingdom goals. To each of these temptations, Jesus said *no*. Jesus refused to use wrong means for good, worthy ends.

Jesus' approach to evangelism was related to his understanding of God. In the pictures of God which Jesus gave us in the parables of Luke 15, we have God first of all pictured as the Good Shepherd pursuing one lost sheep. Ninety-nine sheep are safe, but God is not satisfied with that. He goes out and faces great danger to bring home the one lost sheep. In matters of salvation, the initiative is always with the Lord. He is a seeking God.

In the story of the prodigal son, Jesus pictured God as a loving father who allowed his younger son to go into the far country. The father granted his son the freedom to do what was wrong and hurtful. Yet the father never stopped caring. Jesus told his listeners that the father saw the son when he was "a long way off." This brief description tells us volumes about God. God loves and respects his creatures so much that he does not force them to come home. Yet his love is so great that he is constantly looking for the return of the lost child.

Conversion happens when the prodigal comes to his senses, consciously realizes who he is, what he is becoming, and decides, *I will go to my father.*

Conversion is a matter of the heart. We can't force others into the kingdom of God. As Christ's representatives on earth, we're to tell the good news. We are to give ourselves to other people in love, and we are to pray; but we cannot force erring children to come back to the Father.

Although the New Testament doesn't use the words *soul freedom,* that's exactly what we see in the story of the prodigal son. God allows his children the freedom even to do wrong. It is only in allowing this that true love is possible. If we were robots controlled by God, our response to him would not be one of love. What God most wants is for us to want to love him fully and freely. This notion of soul freedom is the very core of the heritage we've received as Baptists.

Dr. E. Y. Mullins, distinguished Southern Baptist theologian, wrote in *The Axioms of Religion* "that the doctrine of the soul's competency in religion under God is the *historical* significance of the Baptists." This doctrine "assumes that man is made in God's image and that God is a person able to reveal himself to man."[2]

Implications of Soul Freedom

Soul freedom or the competency of the soul in religion implies the following Baptist distinctives having to do with our renewal as a people of God.

1. Regenerate church membership. Being a Christian is a conscious, voluntary matter. Baptists view the authentic church as made up of those believers who have consciously and freely said *yes* to God's mercy and trusted themselves to him in Christ. A person is not born a Christian. Neither family heritage nor the state can make a person a Christian. We as Baptists should move toward restoring an authentic experience of regenerate church membership.

2. Believer's baptism. Being baptized is an act to be entered into by a responsible person on a voluntary basis. Baptism doesn't save. But it is an act of obedience to Christ, a symbol of the believer's passage from death to new life in Christ. Since babies are not responsible persons who can understand what they are doing, Baptists don't baptize infants.

In 1609 John Smyth, Thomas Helwys, and about forty other English Separatists formed a new church in Amsterdam. It was likely the first English-speaking Baptist church formed on the basis of believer's baptism. In 1612 Helwys led the church back to England and established the first Baptist church on English soil at Spitalfields just outside London.

3. The priesthood of believers. If every person has direct access to God through Jesus Christ, there is no need for an earthly priesthood of the kind that we see under the Old Covenant. All believers are priests—for themselves, for other believers, and to people outside the church. Each believer is responsible to do God's work in the world and to give an account of himself to God. Each believer should be encouraged to recognize his gifts and to use those gifts in preaching, teaching, ministering, giving, and witnessing.

In connection with this distinctive, there are two temptations we should encourage each other to avoid. One temptation is to be innovative and individualistic, regardless of how the innovation accords with biblical teaching. The second temptation is to get locked into particular interpretations of biblical teachings which cause us to ignore the powerful implications of the priesthood of believers.

4. Democratic polity. If individuals are competent before God and the church is composed of regenerate members, it follows that the church is a spiritual democracy. Regenerate members are those who have placed the will of Christ above their own wills. They recognize that Christ is the Lord of the church and that he is able to communicate his will through his people, the church.

In practice, a Baptist church appears to be a democracy. But where the church is truly the church, democracy is only the means of seeking the will of Christ. However, this doesn't mean that every vote expresses the will of Christ.

The growing gap between leaders and followers is having the effect that the followers are weakened spiritually because they are not encouraged to claim their God-given birthright of spiritual freedom. They become overly dependent on their spiritual leaders. What would we think of parents who thought they should feed their child nothing but milk when the child was five or six years old? Or what would we think of parents who were so protective of their children that they would not allow them to exercise their muscles and learn to walk. The very thought of this is appalling to us. And yet, if we think about the way we relate to fellow believers in Christ, we may find that we are keeping them from exercising their souls in relating to God.

5. Church autonomy. Each local congregation is autonomous under the lordship of Christ. Authority is vested in Christ as understood by the congregation as a whole—not in the minister, not in a few church leaders.

Each Baptist church governs its own affairs. No Baptist has authority over another. Baptists are bound together by covenants and commitments entered into voluntarily.

Today, as in times past among Southern Baptists, there is a tendency to ignore this important part of our heritage. There is a temptation to use coercion and power politics to guide the direction of Baptist life. This approach may be expedient and successful in the short run. But where this happens, the church as a whole is weakened.

We are fond of saying, "You can lead Baptists but you cannot drive them." Where you have Baptists who know and claim their heritage, this is true. But today many Baptists don't claim their heritage because they don't even know it. If we are to experience renewal as individuals, as churches, and as a denomination, we must help our people become aware of their spiritual birthright and help them to claim it and live it out.

6. Religious liberty for all. Baptists have been champions and shapers of religious liberty for all, believers and nonbelievers, Baptists, Protestants, Catholics, Jews, sects, and even those who claim to be atheists. This concept grows out of the Baptist understanding of soul competency, salvation by grace alone, and the priesthood of believers.

When the Constitution of the United States was adopted in 1787, it did not include sufficient safeguards for religious freedom. Isaac Backus (1724-1806), an itinerant Baptist preacher, rallied Baptists throughout the colonies by sermons, tracts, and political lobbying. Another Baptist, John Leland (1754-1841),

Encouraging counsel to the Southern Baptist family:

Let us quit trying to make creedalists and get on with the Great Commission.
Grady C. Cothen, President, BSSB, 1975-1984

We must come back to adequate counseling of the convert, a solid follow-up program, Christian growth, and churchmanship. We must return to the teaching and preaching of the great doctrines of our faith.
Roy Edgemon, Dir., Church Training Department, BSSB

I have a great concern that young pastors understand our heritage and history. . . . Let's set our minds on missions, evangelism, and stewardship, and the Father will double this great denomination in our lifetime.
R. B. Haygood, Exec. Dir.-Treas., Indiana

When we let the old concept of Baptist Training Union die, we lost our agency for teaching Baptist doctrine. Thus, we have reared a generation which lacks understanding of the people called *Southern Baptists.* We need to teach intensively who we are and what we believe.
Herschel H. Hobbs, President, SBC, 1962-1964

A sense of history, a greater awareness of how God has moved among Southern Baptists in the past is vital to the success of Bold Mission Thrust. An understanding of Baptist heritage is a vital resource for restoring identity, solving current problems, and planning for the future.
Lynn E. May, Jr., Exec. Dir.-Treas., Historical Commission, SBC

From the beginning our purpose has been "for eliciting, combining, and directing the energies of the Baptist denomination of Christians for the propagation of the gospel." The Cooperative Program enables us to do this.
Roy W. Owen, Exec. Dir., Northern Plains

The doctrine of the priesthood of the believer needs to be acknowledged with a higher New Testament priority in order to create the climate in which we can enjoy unity and diversity.
Ray P. Rust, Exec. Sec.-Treas., South Carolina

greatly influenced James Madison, the principal author of the Bill of Rights.

As Walter Shurden has shown, these weren't isolated heroes. They both worked within the framework of the Baptist denomination—primarily Baptist associations.[3] Historians have largely credited Baptists for the First Amendment to the Constitution, "Congress shall make no law respecting an establishment of religion, or prohibiting the free exercise thereof."

Renewal of this Baptist distinctive is needed today. Persecution, coercion, and government sponsorship are not the Baptist ways of advancing the kingdom of God. Our generation of Baptists must continue to proclaim and practice the liberty of all to believe or not believe in the God and Father of our Lord Jesus Christ. For good reasons we are desperately concerned about the moral and spiritual quality of life in our nation. We Baptists can respond with renewed zeal in at least three ways:

(1) Strong resistance to the establishment of secularism as the religion of the land with favored treatment of secularism by all government bodies;

(2) Resistance to the efforts of those who would advance the Christian faith by government approval at the sacrifice of freedom of conscience of unbelieving Americans;

(3) Changing the direction of our nation by authentic Christian methods of evangelism, ministry, and ethical behavior.

7. Separation of church and state. A free church in a free state has been an unwavering commitment of Baptists since their beginnings in seventeenth-century England. Derived from the nature of the gospel, as well as soul freedom, Baptists have held that the state has no authority in the church and that the church has no authority over the state.

Baptists must continue to resist the encroachment of the government at all levels into the affairs of the church and the encroachment of the church into the affairs of state. Throughout Baptist life, we must resist the temptation to use the organized strength of the churches and their agencies to accomplish political ends. The pressures of our American society seem to threaten the purest expression of this ideal. We do not believe in the separation of God and government, but we do believe in the separation of tax support and the kingdom work of Christ. "Render to Caesar the things that are Caesar's; and to God the things that are God's" (Luke 20:25). That is the foundation for our renewal in this Baptist distinctive.

The Modern Missions Movement

The emphases which flow from the realization of soul freedom before God are part of a heritage owned by Baptists worldwide. Not long after Baptists came on the scene, another emphasis joined the stream which would later become part of the rich heritage of Southern Baptists.

Baptists became part of and eventually leaders in the modern missions movement. William Carey, who became a Baptist at the age of eighteen, wouldn't have claimed for himself the title that later generations have given him—"the father of modern missions." Stephen Neill wrote in *A History of Christian Missions*, "Carey stood, and was conscious of standing, in a noble succession as the heir of many pioneers in the past. Yet his work does represent a turning point; it marks the entry of the English-speaking world on a large scale into the missionary enterprise."

In the closing years of the eighteenth century, Carey faced a form of hyper-Calvinism that reasoned that whenever God wanted to convert the heathen he would do it in his own way. Nothing human beings could do would hasten it.

As Carey studied his Bible and the world of his time, he became convicted that it is the duty of Christians to proclaim the gospel to the ends of the earth. On May 31, 1792, Carey addressed a group of Baptist ministers at Nottingham, beginning with the text from Isaiah 54:2-3. From this Carey presented his twofold approach to missions, "Attempt great things for God; expect great things from God."

Four months later the Baptist Society for Propagating the Gospel Among the Heathen was organized. Carey volunteered to go to India, sailing with his family June 13, 1793. He devoted forty-one of his seventy-three years to India without returning to England. William Carey inspired countless others. Adoniram and Ann Judson together with Luther Rice were used of God to stir Baptists in America in a unified mission effort. The Judsons and Rice sailed to India as Congregational missionaries. As they studied the New Testament aboard ship, they accepted the Baptist position of believer's baptism by immersion. The Judsons went to Burma to begin work while Rice returned to the United States to organize united Baptist support for overseas missions. Baptists responded to Rice, and the Baptist heritage of missions expanded from England to the United States.

In May 1814 the Triennial Convention was organized by thirty-three Baptist delegates from eleven states meeting in Philadelphia. This cooperative effort grew out of the travels and leadership of Luther Rice along the Eastern Seaboard. Luther Rice was chosen to serve as the agent for this Baptist body, and the Judsons were appointed as missionaries. A number of streams of the Baptist heritage came together in this effort, and the work of Baptists in America began to grow.

Southern Baptist Convention

The streams of soul freedom and Christian missions flowed together on May 8, 1845, as about 290 Baptist delegates from across the South gathered at the First Baptist Church of Augusta, Georgia, representing over 365,000 Baptists. The Southern Baptist Convention was formed, and a new era in Baptist work began. The convention method of unified missionary work was deliberately chosen over the existing society plan.[4] The convention approach was expressed in a persuasive way in former times by Richard Furman and guided by William B. Johnson, first president of the Southern Baptist Convention.

The first Southern Baptists turned away from separate societies for doing Christian work, choosing instead to follow a more co-operative pattern of one general convention closely related to the churches for all Christian ministries. A board of managers was selected to supervise foreign missions and another for domestic missions. Other boards were later created by the Convention.

Denominational unity was encouraged by the nature of this new convention structure, and yet the autonomy of the local churches was preserved. In its very beginning, the fledgling Southern Baptist Convention was formed by Baptists from four distinct traditions. These four traditions have been recently described by Walter Shurden as follows:

1. The Charleston tradition, characterized by order in theology, church government, worship, and in valuing education for ministers.

2. The Sandy Creek tradition (North Carolina), expressed in ardor of revivalism, personal evangelism, inspired leadership. In this tradition, theology was thoroughly biblical and ecclesiology was highly independent.

3. The Georgian tradition, emphasizing sectionalism, denominational consciousness, and cooperative effort.

4. The Tennessee tradition, centered around the historical Baptist successionism as the only valid churches and the emphasis on the local church, its ordinances and ministry.[5]

Little wonder that the Southern Baptist Convention has had from the beginning its strong personalities in leadership and its controversial issues. But there has been the great unifying factor of the Convention. Historians have generally agreed that the structure which was missionary rather than doctrinal, the two mission boards, and the other institutions created brought about the unifying force in the denomination.

The creation of the second Sunday School Board in 1891 under the inspiration and leadership of J. M. Frost has been another significant factor in unifying the work of the denomination.

The Place of Purpose

I have shown the relationship of heritage and purpose in the New Testament and have looked briefly at the heritage of soul freedom and missionary zeal as they have come together in the formation of the Southern Baptist Convention. We have a rich inheritance. How will we use it? What will we do with it? Those are questions we can't avoid. This is our time, our hour.

Those who have gone before have not only drawn on the heritage passed on to them but they have also been people of great purpose. It is clear that the greatest human accomplishments are made where there is the motivating power of a fundamental mission or purpose. This is true in the life of an individual, a family, an educational institution, a business enterprise, a local church, or in the Southern Baptist denomination.

The renewing power of the denomination's purpose was on my mind on one occasion as I traveled to a state convention assignment. I began reading an article about the National Bureau of Standards mundanely establishing the precise length of a foot, the exact volume of a gallon of liquid, and the unvarying weight of a pound of potatoes. Then, this sentence leaped out at me: "Measurement is *the* mission of the Bureau." That's it! The bureau's primary mission is to maintain and improve the nation's measurement standards.

This insight forced me to ask, Can I succinctly state the purpose of our Baptist people? Can my fellow Southern Baptists do so?

A statement of purpose is one of the most valuable assets of any well-run company. What Peter Drucker, a master craftsman in business management, has written about a business is equally true of our Southern Baptist denomination: "Only a clear definition of the mission and purpose of the business makes possible clear and realistic business objectives. It is the foundation for priorities, strategies, plans, and work assignments. It is the starting point for the design of managerial jobs and, above all, for the design of managerial structures. Structure follows strategy. Strategy determines what the key activities are in a given business. And strategy requires knowing 'what our business is and what it should be.'"[6]

Writing in a time of great denominational tension, E. Y. Mullins said: "Denominational self-respect, a sense of divine calling and mission, must possess any religious body which counts for much in the world. The prophetic mood, which implies that the soul is conquered by some great truth or truths and seeks passionately and restlessly to propagate those truths, is a prime condition of power."[7]

Southern Baptist Purpose Yesterday and Today

The small group of Baptists who gathered in Augusta, Georgia, back in 1845 were people of purpose. Their expression of purpose and a commitment to action are part of a rich heritage that has been passed on from generation to generation even to this hour.

Those who framed the statement of purpose in Augusta could not have envisioned the lines of development that the denomination would take. They could not have possibly foreseen the number of entities that would be required to carry out such a great purpose. But the purpose they framed has become a classic Baptist expression of the reason for our existence. What is perhaps needed most today is for us to lift it up from the pages of our constitution, rescue it from its enshrinement in antiquity, and let it flame in our midst during these crucial days of change and challenge.

The Southern Baptist Convention constitution has this statement of purpose in article 2: "It is the purpose of the Convention to provide a general organization for Baptists in the United States and its territories for the promotion of Christian missions at home and abroad and any other objects such as Christian education, benevolent enterprises, and social services which it may deem proper and advisable for the furtherance of the Kingdom of God."

Bold Mission Thrust

The mission of Southern Baptists has come to have a contemporary expression in the last decade in what is called Bold Mission Thrust. A network of broad objectives and priorities has been stated in such a way as to elicit the support of Southern Baptist people across our country. It has to one degree or another gained the support of multitudes of our churches, associations, state conventions, institutions, and agencies. The goal set forth in Bold Mission Thrust is that everyone in the world may have an opportunity to hear and accept the gospel of Christ by AD 2000.

This purpose has to some degree succeeded. But Bold Mission Thrust has yet to have its most powerful renewing effect on Southern Baptists. This really is our great mission, and we as the denomination must continue to say so with unity of heart and soul, with resources and programs, with vision and action—agency by agency, association by association, state by state, church by church, Baptist by Baptist. This captivating dream will make a mighty difference among our people and in our world. It is worthy of the zeal and support of every Southern Baptist.

When Norman W. Cox wrote his study course book, *We Southern Baptists,* in 1961, he expressed what is most distinctive about being a Baptist in the following way: "It is their concept of redeemed personality ministering under the Lordship of Jesus Christ"[8] as revealed in the Scriptures. The redeemed personality is first and foremost a personality that has received in spite of being unworthy of the gift. Reception of the gift and heritage create a great sense of purpose. And so, through the redeemed Christian, the message and work of grace is transmitted from person to person, from family to family, from nation to nation.

As Southern Baptists we have been given much. Let us more fully appropriate the riches of God's mercy in Christ. Let us also receive with a deep sense of thanks the precious heritage of soul freedom that our fathers and mothers have paid for—some with great cost. As we value, enlarge, and live our heritage, our purpose will be clear and strong. We shall then be equipped to work the works of him who has sent us—while it is day.

Notes

1. J. Kent Carathers and Gary B. Lott, *Mission Review: Foundation for Strategic Planning* (Boulder, CO: National Center for Higher Education Management Systems, 1981), p. 1.

2. E. Y. Mullins, *The Axioms of Religion* (Philadelphia: The Judson Press, 1908), pp. 56, 58.

3. Walter B. Shurden, "The Great Man Myth—Baptists and Religious Liberty: Associational Activities Before 1814," *The Quarterly Review,* 40, No. 3 (April-June, 1980), pp. 51-58.

4. For a clear statement of the differences between the society method and the convention method of organization, see James L. Sullivan, *Baptist Polity As I See It* (Nashville: Broadman Press, 1983), pp. 33-34, 85-93.

5. Walter B. Shurden, "The Southern Baptist Synthesis: Is It Cracking?" *Baptist History and Heritage,* XVI, No. 2 (April, 1981), pp. 2-11.

6. Peter F. Drucker, *Management: Tasks, Responsibilities, Practices* (New York: Harper & Row Publishers, Inc., 1974), p. 75.

7. Mullins, pp. 19-20.

8. Norman W. Cox, *We Southern Baptists* (Nashville: Convention Press, 1961), p. 4.

3
Biblical
Beliefs

Challenge #3: As a people of God, let us recognize the importance of a central core of shared beliefs, base them on biblical authority, and confess them freely under the lordship of Christ.

Galatians 1:6-7: I am amazed that you are so quickly deserting Him who called you by the grace of Christ, for a different gospel; which is really not another; only there are some who are disturbing you, and want to distort the gospel of Christ.
2 Corinthians 3:17: Now the Lord is the Spirit; and where the Spirit of the Lord is, there is liberty.

The Importance of Doctrine: Many people today have little patience with any kind of definite doctrinal teaching in religion. This aversion to religious doctrine is not confined to those who are altogether indifferent or hostile to religion. Even many religious people are unfriendly toward any kind of definite doctrinal teaching. . . . A religion without doctrine would be a religion without meaning. Such a religion could be neither propagated nor defended. . . . The element of doctrine in Christianity, then, is necessary. To talk about religion without doctrine is to talk nonsense. Of course, this is not to say that doctrine is all that there is in religion. It is possible to overemphasize the place of doctrine. We need to remember, also, that doctrine does not exist for its own sake; it is not something to be held in the mind and thought about only. It is a program of activity. The whole New Testament emphasizes the fact that to hear the Word is not enough; it must be put into action. Doctrine is not a system of ideas to be contemplated only; it is a call to life and activity. One must not only hear the Word; one must also do it. But, we repeat, doctrine is necessary or our activity is blind and purposeless.

W. T. CONNER[1]

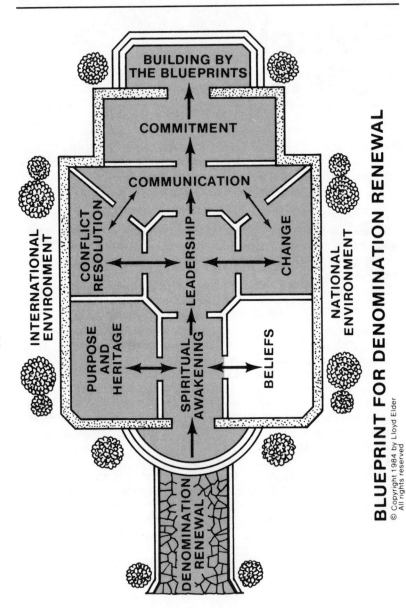

BLUEPRINT FOR DENOMINATION RENEWAL

Beliefs are for many at the heart of the present troubled times among Southern Baptists. This is not surprising. Southern Baptists have been and are a people for whom beliefs matter. Our firm convictions have been one of our stabilizing strengths as a people of God. As I observed in the preceding chapter, many of our Baptist forebears suffered and some died for convictions at the heart of the gospel.

In the present controversy, two time-honored Baptist convictions are being pitted against each other. *The first conviction is that our doctrine should be pure.* Baptists have believed historically that the Bible is the single, primary, complete, and authoritative foundation for our beliefs. We have believed that our own opinions, understandings, and statements need to be aligned with and formed from the Word of God.

This concern for purity of doctrine isn't a recent one. Let me add that neither is it theoretical. It has been of personal concern for my own life for three decades. In the New Testament era, the concern to separate sound from unsound doctrine was expressed almost from the very beginning. In some religions, doctrines don't matter very much. Some religions, by their very nature, are able to tolerate all kinds of beliefs and doctrine. Not so Christianity.

One of the earliest Christian writings was Paul's letter to the Galatians. Paul wrote this letter in a white heat. Some religious teachers were claiming that for Gentiles to be saved, they had to become Jews. In order to become Jews, they had to go through certain Jewish rituals. So, according to those teachers, Gentiles were saved by grace *plus* ceremonial rituals.

Paul argued in the Galatian letter that grace plus anything else is not grace. Once you understand the nature of God's grace, you see that adding anything to grace makes it less than grace. Either God saves by grace or he doesn't. Our belief about this will have far-reaching implications for how we relate to God and to other human beings.

From Paul's heated letter to the Galatians down to our own day, beliefs have mattered and do matter. They shape who we are and who we will become both in this world and in the world to come. They determine how we relate to God, to each other, to ourselves, and to our work for the Lord.

A second Baptist conviction, which at times seems to collide with the belief that doctrine should be pure, *is the priesthood of all believers,* also called *soul freedom.* Most Baptists have believed from the beginning that authentic faith is something that cannot be coerced by any human authority. We believe that all persons are free before God and are accountable to God for how they relate to him and for how they interpret and obey his Word, the Bible.

In our present debate, those most at odds are likely to put more weight on one of these two historic Baptist convictions than on the other. Good brethren disagree. There is no question but that these arguments over doctrine can be used as a lightning rod to strike at other agendas within the denomination. Concern over doctrinal purity or concern over soul liberty can arise from motives that are far from pure. Even so, there is something important that we should learn from this controversy. We need to listen carefully, with discernment, to see what is being said and why.

I don't believe that doctrinal purity and soul liberty are incompatible with each other. I believe we can have both. In fact, if we're going to be true to the Word of God, we will not neglect either of these convictions.

How can we do this? How can we as Southern Baptists move in the direction that affirms the vital necessity of sound doctrine and yet allows each individual to appropriate his beliefs from the Word of God? How can we respond in such a way that our shared beliefs become a part of our denomination renewal instead of contributing to our fragmentation?

There are some things we can do. Now what I suggest is not *what* Southern Baptists should believe. No Baptist could do that for another. Rather, I would like to suggest some ways for us to deal with our doctrines and with one another so that we can build strength upon strength in being a people of God and in doing his work in the world.

1. *Let us affirm that our doctrinal beliefs do matter—that they are important in every area of life.* Our lives, our actions, our attitudes, and our choices constantly reveal what we really believe. Every choice we make shows what we consider to be the most important thing at that time. What do our actions and choices show about what we really believe? Do they reveal that our minds (including what we believe) are being conformed to the image of Christ, that we are putting on the mind of Christ? Our appropriation of Christian beliefs has an important part in God's work of conforming us to the image of Christ, in creating the mind of Christ within us. If we take biblical doctrine lightly, we shall hinder the work of God in our own lives and in the lives of his churches.

2. *Let us accept the lordship of Christ as the norm for all Christian doctrine and our understanding of the nature of revelation.* If you've ever been outside on a dark night when a thunderstorm passed through, you know that the landscape looks different when the sky lights up. For just a moment, everything is clear. The entire landscape is transformed.

Something like that has happened in the life, death, and resurrection of Jesus. Who of us wouldn't like to have been on the road to Emmaus with Cleopas and his friend? As they left Jerusalem with their spirits drooping, they had no idea that their entire understanding of God in history would be changed before the end of the day.

A stranger approached. He didn't seem to know what everyone in Jerusalem had been talking about. Cleopas told him what had just happened to Jesus of Nazareth.

Then Jesus, still not recognized, said, " 'O foolish men and slow of heart to believe in all that the prophets have spoken! Was it not necessary for the Christ to suffer these things and enter into His glory?' And beginning with Moses and with all the prophets, He explained to them the things concerning Himself in all the Scriptures" (Luke 24:25-27).

Then in a later meeting with the eleven, the risen Lord appeared and said to them, " 'These are My words which I spoke to you while I was still with you, that all things which are written about Me in the Law of Moses and the Prophets and the Psalms must be fulfilled.' Then He opened their minds to understand the Scriptures" (Luke 24:44-45). As Christ opened the minds of the disciples to understand the Scriptures, so he is our Guide and Light in reading and obeying Scripture today.

3. *Let us acknowledge the Bible as the single, primary, complete, and authoritative foundation for our beliefs.* Christian faith means that God has most fully revealed himself in history in the person of his Son, Jesus of Nazareth. Something once and for all, not to be repeated, has been done. The apostles, those eyewitnesses of what God did in Christ, are dead. But in the writings we call the New Testament, the apostles left their Spirit-inspired witness to the saving, revealing events which they saw and heard. It is only through their writings that we have access to these events. We know of Christ only through Scripture.

Jesus accepted as authoritative Scripture the writings which we now call the Old Testament. The apostles accepted these as authoritative and inspired Scriptures. Paul affirmed that all of these Scriptures were inspired by God.

Since the close of the apostolic era, Christians have produced a large body of literature besides the Old and New Testaments. These works contain much wisdom and excellent writing. But, none of these writings can ever claim the kind of authority that Holy Scripture has.

4. *Let us draw upon appropriate resources for our doctrinal beliefs as supportive and secondary.* I have already affirmed that Scripture is the primary source of authority for the churches. Many of our differences stem from the fact that we have different backgrounds and different understandings. We bring our various

Encouraging counsel to the Southern Baptist family:

We need to rediscover the joy of our salvation, enthrone Jesus Christ as Lord in our lives, actually practice Bible and doctrine study, and get on with the task of sharing our faith with a lost, hungry, and dying world.
James W. Clark, Exec. V. Pres., BSSB

We cannot claim we believe in biblical authority and in the supremacy of Jesus Christ and at the same time deny what he believed about biblical authority. This is the major problem in our Southern Baptist Convention academia today.
James T. Draper, President, SBC, 1982-1984

Remember that our fellowship and our mission commitment are not dependent upon our cultural tastes, our provincialism, or our worship style but upon the commonality of our redemption in Christ!
Wes Forbis, Secretary, Church Music Department, BSSB

Hold fast our worthy Baptist heritage, love one another, press on together, claiming the gospel, sharing the faith, ministering in Jesus' name, and growing churches of the Lord in every community throughout the world.
Robert L. Lee, Exec. Dir., Louisiana

We must saturate our denomination with basics. Those basics are the acceptance, proclamation, and application of the biblical revelation that Jesus Christ died, was buried, and rose again so that people throughout the world might have life.
Morton F. Rose, V. Pres., Church Programs and Services, BSSB

Let's have a rebirth in the confidence, in the total reliability of the Bible. Let us once again hear terms like "burden for a lost world," "soul-winning," "Holy Ghost revival," and "men are lost apart from Jesus."
Bailey E. Smith, President, SBC, 1980-1982

By this shall all men know that you are my disciples, if you have love for one another (John 13:35).
David P. Turner, Dir., Management Services Division, BSSB

understandings to the reading of Scripture. What we bring to the reading of Scripture will in some way affect how we understand what the Bible is saying. If that were not so, we would all agree on what the Bible says. While each of us should give ourselves to studying the Word of God directly, we can add to and enrich the understanding that we bring to our reading of the Bible.

Knowing more about the history of the church can give us a broader perspective of where we now are as a people of God. Learning something about how Christians in times past sought to formulate their beliefs can help us as we wrestle with our own beliefs.

It would be helpful for each of us to look at various creeds and confessions of faith that Christians have produced. Although without any authority over Baptists today, these are attempts of Christians at various times in their history to summarize what they believe. Those expressions of faith called *creeds* were formulated before the Protestant Reformation. They became the standards of belief. *Confessions,* on the other hand, were statements of belief formulated after Christendom divided into denominations. In many cases, these creeds and confessions have been used to coerce people to believe a certain way. Despite the fact that these human statements of Christian belief have been misused, summarizing Christian doctrines has value for our expressing what beliefs we hold in common. Those who formulated "The Baptist Faith and Message," which was adopted by the Southern Baptist Convention of 1963, made clear the confessional nature of this statement of faith in the introduction.

As Baptists, we would do well to study the writings of Baptist theologians. These people don't have the authority of the Bible. But they have devoted their lives to understanding God's revelation in Christ. While these theologians can't make our journeys for us, they can help point out some of the thickets and quicksand so we may get on with our journeys.

Also, we would do well as Southern Baptists to go back and look at the doctrinal study books we have produced and have used to train our people in their beliefs. A marvelous consistency of belief can be found in books of this kind.

5. *Let us cling to the great strength that lies in a central core of shared biblical doctrine.* I've mentioned the function of creeds, confessions, and a core of shared beliefs evident in our books designed to instruct in doctrine. If you compared creeds, confessions, and doctrinal study books, you would find a basic core of shared beliefs about which there has been little controversy among Baptists and many other Christians from various traditions. These core beliefs form the gospel. When one such belief is denied, a harmful effect is produced on the rest of the core beliefs. By this I mean certain doctrines are interrelated. For example, to deny the resurrection of Christ is to cast doubt on the claim that he died for our sins. The earliest witnesses understood this quite clearly. Paul said if Christ had not been raised from the dead then the apostolic preaching was empty, and worse, that it was a fake, a misrepresentation of what God had done. Not only that but also those who believed in Christ were still in their sins (1 Cor. 15:12-19).

6. *Let us resist the practice of making every doctrinal difference a test of fellowship.* There should be room for interpretive diversity of those beliefs that are not a part of our core beliefs. This doesn't mean that these doctrines are not important. It does mean that devout Christians can disagree on them without breaking their fellowship and without denying the gospel itself.

For example, one core belief is that Christ is coming again. If you look in the major creeds, confessions, and doctrinal teachings of the churches, you will find this belief. What is not so universally accepted is the relationship of Christ's second coming to the millennium. Given the same biblical data, devout Christians have interpreted in diverse manners the second coming of Christ in relationship to the millennium. Among Southern Baptists the return of Christ is held as a central, core belief, but the millennium has not been a test of fellowship.

7. *Let us adopt a confessional rather than dogmatic stance*

within the denomination in matters related to doctrine. By *confessional stance,* I mean let us freely and gladly express our beliefs and allow others to do the same. Let us allow our churches to formulate their own confessions and covenants. Let no church or individual impose upon others a humanly constructed statement or interpretation of our biblical faith. At the denominational level, the churches and individual Southern Baptists have a right to expect that Convention agencies will do their work according to guidelines of a common confession of faith that has survived the test of time and is at the central core of biblical faith.

It would be most unwise and even harmful to divide and dismantle the strength of the denomination over doctrinal issues that are private and open to various interpretations. It would be just as unwise to act as if doctrine does not matter to Bible-believing people.

8. *Let us learn valuable lessons from brethren who call out to us from the extreme left or the extreme right, but let us not follow them.* There will always be extreme positions among Southern Baptists; our freedom not only permits but also encourages it. But our strength has been and will continue to be the fact that a large portion of our people hold a central core of shared beliefs and values. We as Southern Baptists will defend a person's right to deny the authority of the Bible or to reject a central Christian belief, but such a person would not be acceptable to most Southern Baptists in a denominational leadership role or on a local church staff.

On the other hand, most Southern Baptists do not want to be badgered and pushed around by fellow Baptists on a crusade to clean house and get rid of all hints of doctrinal diversity.

As for me, I want to spend my life and energy as a follower of Christ, responding to him and to his revelation in Holy Scripture, not in trying to prove some fellow Baptist wrong or even trying to prove that I am this, that, or the other. But for the record, mark me down as one among a vast number of Southern Baptists who is "middle of the road" and biblically conservative. Most Southern

Baptists are biblical conservatives. They are not merely logical fundamentalists, practical moderates, or philosophical liberals. The sooner we recognize that and act on it, the better it will be for our fellowship and our work.

9. *Let us practice the discipline of confessing the faith we hold in biblical terms rather than in terms that reflect party lines and party spirit.* A large majority of Southern Baptists would undoubtedly affirm the following Scriptures which either initially or in their full meaning speak of Holy Scripture.

Thy word I have treasured in my heart,/That I may not sin against Thee (Ps. 119:11).

I shall keep Thy statutes;/Do not forsake me utterly!/How can a young man keep his way pure?/By keeping it according to Thy word (Ps. 119:8-9).

Forever, O Lord,/Thy word is settled in heaven (Ps. 119:89).

Thy word is a lamp to my feet,/And a light to my path (Ps. 119:105).

The grass withers, the flower fades,/But the word of our God stands forever (Isa. 40:8).

Do not think that I came to abolish the Law or the Prophets; I did not come to abolish, but to fulfill. For truly I say to you, until heaven and earth pass away, not the smallest letter or stroke shall pass away from the Law, until all is accomplished (Matt. 5:17-18).

You search the Scriptures, because you think that in them you have eternal life; and it is these that bear witness of Me (John 5:39).

God, after He spoke long ago to the fathers in the prophets in many portions and in many ways, in these last days has spoken to us in His Son, whom He appointed heir of all things, through whom also He made the world (Heb. 1:1-2).

For the word of God is living and active and sharper than any two-edged sword, piercing as far as the division of soul and spirit, of both joints and marrow, and able to judge the thoughts and intentions of the heart (Heb. 4:12).

And so we have the prophetic word made more sure, to which you do well to pay attention as to a lamp shining in a dark place, until the day dawns and the morning star arises in your hearts. But know this first of all, that no prophecy of Scripture is a matter of one's own interpretation, for no prophecy was ever made by an act of human will, but men moved by the Holy Spirit spoke from God (2 Pet. 1:19-21).

That from childhood you have known the sacred writings which are able to give you the wisdom that leads to salvation through faith which is in Christ Jesus. All Scripture is inspired by God and profitable for teaching, for reproof, for correction, for training in righteousness; that the man of God may be adequate, equipped for every good work (2 Tim. 3:15-17).

The vast majority of Southern Baptists would affirm what the Bible says about itself. But there are a number of ways different individuals could take these biblical quotes and from them construct a theory of inspiration and authority. This we must allow. In searching for a theory of inspiration, many other Scriptures would have to be taken into account. Also, we would want to consult church history, historical theology, Baptist theologians, and the creeds and confessions of the church. But ultimately, we must leave the individual with his open Bible before the living God who created him. The individual is responsible to God alone for his interpretation of the Bible. He alone is responsible for how he relates to God.

What an impact these Scriptures above have had on us as Southern Baptists! We affirm that God inspired Holy Scripture. But exactly how he did it is a matter of some interpretation.

The statement of our belief about Holy Scriptures from what Scripture says about itself provides for Southern Baptists a platform that is deep, wide, and solid. The Bible is inspired, divine, human, spiritual, practical, experiential, perfect, salvational, and eternal.

Hopefully these nine suggestions will help to guide Southern Baptists in a direction that claims with integrity our heritage, our freedom, our accountability to God. We can respond in such a way that our shared beliefs become a part of our denomination renewal instead of our fragmentation.

Denomination renewal then depends largely on how we handle our approach to beliefs. Any effective, productive organization has a common core of shared beliefs. If the shared beliefs are too detailed and brittle, then the organization is limited in the number and kinds of people it can attract to its cause. The result is that the cohesive power in shared beliefs becomes a divisive, fragmenting force.

But if shared beliefs are indeed central, lofty, and self-evident to a large number in the organization, there is an overwhelming sense of commitment and loyalty generated among the people.

Effective organizations know what they stand for—what matters—what is worth the battle; and they don't stop to argue about it all the time.

As an effective, renewed, and renewing denomination, we can move on to our greatest contribution both within and outside the family of God if we recognize the mighty force of our convictions and beliefs.

The two great convictions presented in this chapter stand supporting each other, not opposing each other. (1) It does matter what we believe as Southern Baptists, and (2) each Southern Baptist is free under Christ to hold and confess personal beliefs.

When Christians carefully study the Scriptures under the tutelage of the Holy Spirit, they know in the depths of their beings that this is the Word of God. As we make this discovery firsthand, we find ourselves not worshiping the Bible but being handed over by the Bible into the presence of the living God who is revealed in that Book. We will experience on a daily basis the redeeming work of God's Son, Jesus Christ. Those who find themselves caught up in this redemptive and redeeming activity and become co-workers with God confess freely that it does matter what we believe. But these folk also find it less and less important to argue endlessly over fine points of doctrine.

The history of many churches and some denominations in our own time is a tragic reminder of what an exaggerated concern over fine points of doctrine can do. It leads to party spirit, a spirit of deadness, and a spirit of hostility. On the other hand, Christian history is also filled with evidence of the decline and death of those who did not acknowledge the rightful place of sound doctrine. None of these are the works or fruit of the Holy Spirit.

To those who know firsthand the power of the Word of God, there is no question about its efficacy. Rather than quarrel about the nature of it, they take the sword of the Spirit in hand to do battle against the devil and all his forces which would like to destroy the people of God and hold in bondage the people of this world.

Note

1. W. T. Conner, *Christian Doctrine* (Nashville: Broadman Press, 1937), pp. 11,13,14.

4
Spiritual Awakening

Challenge #4: As a people of God, let us long for a spiritual awakening from God that is kindled by the Holy Spirit and keeps us on the path of biblical faith, that revives the churches, that brings large numbers of new believers into the kingdom of God, and that depends completely on the providence and work of God.

2 Chronicles 7:14: And [if] My people who are called by My name humble themselves and pray, and seek My face and turn from their wicked ways, then I will hear from heaven, will forgive their sin, and will heal their land.

Repentance and Faith: If the world ever needed a spiritual awakening, it is now. The destiny of men and nations and individuals has been changed when men daring to repent of their sins have returned to Jesus Christ by faith. Repentance and faith go hand-in-hand.

BILLY GRAHAM

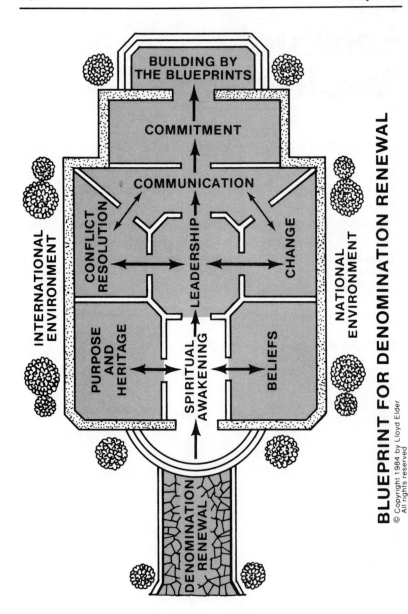

BLUEPRINT FOR DENOMINATION RENEWAL

People on their own cannot blueprint or program spiritual awakening. We all know that. At the same time, human beings, and more specifically, the people of God, have had and even now experience an increased longing for spiritual awakening from God. As part of God's people, we Southern Baptists have a heightened desire for a spiritual awakening.

During my several years of itinerant preaching and recent months of intensive listening, I have heard this theme on every hand. From pastors and laypersons, from college presidents and evangelists, from agency leaders and elected leaders, there is a heart cry for awakening and genuine revival. How desperately we need it—again!

Southern Baptists formally organized in 1845. Since then there have been two major spiritual awakenings in the United States. Both of these awakenings have had an impact on Christians in a variety of denominations.

The first of these was the Prayer Revival of 1858-1859, which both embraced and grew under the ministry of Dwight L. Moody. During this awakening more than 188,000 people were converted and joined Southern Baptist churches—a ratio of one convert to every eleven church members. This compares to our present ratio of one convert to thirty-four members.

Another awakening took place around 1905. It was international in scope. This revival also touched Southern Baptists. Following the 1906 meeting of the Southern Baptist Convention in Chattanooga, Tennessee, the annual report included this description:

> The spirit of evangelism is abroad in the land. From every part of the country there come the tokens of increased revival fervor among the churches of all denominations of Christians. In many of our cities there has been very distinct and extraordinary evangelistic enthusiasm. More people have been reached by the gospel in our great cities through evangelistic agencies in the last year than ever before. Great halls, theaters, skating rinks, and other large central meeting places have been utilized by evangelists, and

thousands of nonchurch-goers have been reached in this way. The country sections and small towns have likewise shared in the evangelistic sweep.[1]

Characteristics of the Great Spiritual Awakenings

What is meant by *spiritual awakening?* And why are God's people showing such an interest in spiritual awakening today?

Historians have sought to tell the story of five great awakenings in modern times. Edwin Orr in his book, *The Flaming Tongue,* defines a spiritual awakening as the movement of the Holy Spirit to bring about a revival of New Testament Christianity. The following common characteristics of such awakenings not only set out our needs, but nurture our hope and our longing:

1. There was a sovereign, inexplicable, providential breakthrough from God in the midst of history. The affairs of people had gone along as usual, including a great moral and spiritual degeneration in the land. Then God did something of such proportion that believers and unbelievers alike attributed it to a breakthrough from God in his redemptive work.

2. In profound dependence on God, there was an extraordinary urgency and intensity in prayer, individually and corporately, on the part of at least some of the people of God and among many unbelievers. The prayer meetings were frequent and largely attended.

3. The churches were revived. The Holy Spirit became sovereign in the churches and among the members. Nominal and wayward members were reclaimed, lay leadership and ministry often flourished, and church attendance greatly increased. And there were times of harmonious interdenominational relationships.

4. The Word of God was proclaimed with authority and heard with reverence. Believers had faith that God would honor his word and touch the hearts of the hearers. There was a notable increase in ministers called and sent forth.

5. The masses were attracted to the gospel, and they heard the

evangelists gladly. Large numbers of conversions among the churchgoing and nonchurchgoing became characteristic, far beyond the normal harvest of evangelistic endeavors.

6. Evangelistic efforts and social action went hand in hand. These two did not war against each other. Rather, a heightened interest in the gospel and in conversion was expressed through individuals and institutions in helping with the common needs of others.

7. Religious themes filled conversation on the streets, in the coffee shops, and in places of business. There was genuine interest in the things of Christ and his church.

8. During the awakenings, there was a revival of righteousness in the land. People became honest, bills were paid, bars were empty, jail cells and courtrooms were not so crowded. Bartenders and distillers often closed down their places of business because of conversion. There was repentance and confession of all sorts of sins. Restitution was often made, and broken relationships in church, home, and business were made right.

9. And finally, the awakenings usually had a lasting impact on the churches, society, and institutions—an impact that could be experienced and assessed for two or more decades.

To know of the time when God has done such a notable and redemptive work among people excites our own longing for a great spiritual awakening among Southern Baptists today! But even more profoundly are we challenged to nurture such a longing because of the instruction and promises of Holy Scripture.

A Great Awakening Text

For many of us, 2 Chronicles 7:14 has become a great awakening text. In it we see a promise of divine mercy, an offer of forgiveness, a formula for revival, a way back to God, a key to national restoration. But let us remember that it was first spoken to King Solomon who was alone in the night with God. The Temple had been planned and prepared for by King David. It was constructed and dedicated by King Solomon. Following the dedication, after the people had gone to their tents happy and joyful, Solomon was enshrouded by the darkness of the night but enlightened by this sacred promise from God:

> [If] My people who are called by My name humble themselves and pray, and seek My face and turn from their wicked ways, then I will hear from heaven, will forgive their sin, and will heal their land.

From the nation of Israel and their dedication of the Temple down to this good hour, there is a need for the people of God and all their institutions and structures to be renewed by the Spirit of God. That includes this great Southern Baptist denomination, its members, its churches, its associations, conventions, institutions, and agencies. Let us look more carefully at this text through the experience of our own denomination today.

A People Called by His Name

Spiritual awakening is promised to the people of God—and so to Southern Baptists.

"[If] My people who are called by My name. . . ."

If is a small but important word. In this verse it links the material in 2 Chronicles 6 and 7 to the promise given in verse 14 of chapter 7. The condition of God's people has never come as a surprise to him. He has always known of their tendency to wander from him. It was almost as if God were saying to Solomon: "I know they will not be faithful. But even in their faithlessness, I love them still."

Because God loved his people so much, he disciplined them in the hope that they would wake up, come to their senses, and return to him. If he withheld rain from their land or if he sent insects to destroy their crops, he did so in order to keep them from falling into a greater evil—spiritual death, separation from their Beloved.

These terrible things might happen. But God wanted Solomon and his people to know of a divine readiness and willingness for relationship. But before we look at this in more detail, we need to ask, Who are God's people?

In this verse "My people" refers to Abraham and his seed. These were the children of Isaac and Jacob. These were the slaves freed from Egypt under Moses' leadership. These were the people who covenanted with God at Sinai, whose children took the Promised Land with Joshua as their leader. These were God's people—not because of any intrinsic merit or worth on their part. No. They were God's people out of his own good pleasure. They were *his* because *he* had chosen them.

God says of his people that they are "called by My name." Another way of translating that phrase is "over whom my name is called." The word "name" in this verse is thought to be derived from an Arabic word which means "to mark" or "to brand." God puts his mark or brand on his people. God's people may be described in many ways. But first and foremost they are *his* people—bearers of his name. As such, they are under his ownership, authority, and power. They are to live out their lives as his very own possession. God protects his people from their enemies. He calls his people to responsibility for carrying out his purposes in the world.

As Southern Baptists, we are not the physical heirs of Abraham. But in Christ we have become God's people. With the coming of the new covenant, being God's people doesn't depend on human will or physical lineage. We have become God's people by a spiritual birth process.

What the apostle Peter said in his first letter applies to all believers—whether Jews or Gentiles:

> But you are a chosen race, a royal priesthood, a holy nation, a people for God's own possession, that you may proclaim the excellencies of Him who has called you out of darkness into His marvelous light; for you once were not a people, but now you are the people of God; you had not received mercy, but now you have received mercy (1 Pet. 2:9-10).

Along with all other people who have been born from above, Southern Baptists are God's own people.

A People Humbled to Pray

Spiritual awakening comes to the people of God who have humbled themselves and who are praying.

"If My people . . . humble themselves and pray."

In the text, "humble" means "to bend the knee," "to be brought low," "to be brought under," "to be subdued." It is related to an Arabic word which means "to fold the wings of a bird." It was first used to describe a condition of life involving poverty, affliction, suffering, or lowliness. Slaves and peasants without wealth or standing were *humbled.* But the word came to refer to a godly character trait—humility, lowliness, utter dependence upon God. Humility was similar to patience or meekness and just the opposite of pride or arrogance. Micah 6:8 sets out the duty of God's people: "To do justice, to love kindness,/And to walk humbly with your God."

In the New Testament era, the Greeks and Romans held as desirable traits pride, position, rank, wealth, and possessions. Then Jesus came meek and lowly, preaching a gospel of humility and dependence upon God. Humility is listed among the virtues of those who are followers of Christ and became one essential requirement: "Humble yourselves, therefore, under the mighty hand of God, that He may exalt you at the proper time" (1 Pet. 5:6). "God is opposed to the proud, but gives grace to the humble" (Jas. 4:6).

Let the pastors and denominational leaders be *humbled to pray.* Martin Luther, the powerful man of faith and leader of the Protestant Reformation, preached a sermon on 1 Peter 5:5 *ff.* in which he expounded, "Therefore, St. Peter exhorts both those who possess something given them from God that they abide by the calling in office, and discharge the same in humility. . . . There are to be among Christians in all conditions, offices, services, exclusively humility and works of Christian love and service."

A people humbled "to pray"; that is the center of the requirements of God. In the great prayer of Temple dedication in 2 Chronicles 6:14-42, Solomon lifted up his hands and his voice to God like an appealing refrain: "If Thy people . . . pray . . . then hear Thou in heaven." *Prayer* in the Old Testament and in the New Testament is very often simply the word *ask, request, implore God's favor,* or *incline toward God.* "Pray" in 2 Chronicles 7:14 is a more difficult word; it is tough, not at all sentimental. Make a critical judgment about life and bring your appeal to God. But the lesson from Scripture is overwhelming. We are to be people humbled to pray, to ask our God for his help and blessing.

I would not claim to be an expert in prayer. Most Southern Baptists I know wouldn't either. But we want to be a people of prayer—people who will not let go until he blesses us. We're not to apologize for asking God to help us and to send a great spiritual awakening.

From the human point of view, it may seem that our desire for spiritual awakening, our longing to pray, is just another human impulse. But from the viewpoint of the Word of God, these are more than just human desires. We reach out to him because he first reached out to us. The longing in us for God is a gift from God—the Spirit of God already at work in us. We can pretend it's not there. We can stifle it. We can crowd it out with good things which are not the best. Or, we can nourish it and let it grow. Peter Taylor Forsyth said that God "stirs and inspires all prayer which finds and moves him. His love provokes our sacred forwardness."

Prayer is not magic. It isn't a human crowbar for prying from God something that he's unwilling to give. No. Prayer is God already at work in us—if only in a small way. Because it is God working in us, Tennyson was right to say that more things are wrought by prayer than this world dreams. Prayer is simply one channel through which God does his work.

Because prayer is God's work, we humans can't fully understand it. But we don't have to. There are people who understand
how food is digested and assimilated by the human body. But
think of the billions of us in the world who don't understand that.
Our ignorance of this doesn't keep us from benefiting from food.

So it is with prayer. We need only respond to the prompting,
the longing to pray. God himself, the Holy Spirit, is our best
teacher in prayer. F. W. Krummacher tells in his autobiography
about a Christian friend whose son fell into the swollen Wupper
River. The father of the boy had never swum before. In this situation, he had no time to learn. He did what most of us would do—
cried for the Lord's help and jumped into the flooded Wupper. To
his own amazement, he swam with great skill and was able to
rescue his son. We may not be skilled in prayer, but we can pray if
we will.

Quite often the Spirit of God uses our own human needs as
springboards to prayer. Charlotte Elliott's profound poem, "Just as
I Am," shows our needs can be the connection to a channel of
God's mercy to us.

> Just as I am, poor, wretched, blind;
>   Sight, riches, healing of the mind,
> Yea, all I need in thee to find,
>   O Lamb of God, I come.

Prayer not only has an impact on the individual praying but
also has social consequences. In our human attempt to explain
how prayer works, we have sometimes resorted to saying that
prayer changes things because it changes the person praying. It
certainly does that, but its effects don't stop there. This truth has
gripped me more and more in recent years. George S. Steward
expresses this truth by saying that "prayer creates a new situation." How it does, I don't know. I don't need to know. I do know
that it is our responsibility to pray—to nourish that longing for
speaking to God. If we do, God will do something new.

I earlier mentioned two of the five great awakenings of the

Encouraging counsel to the Southern Baptist family:

Believe, practice, and celebrate the positive reality of the gospel of Jesus Christ which provides freedom, hope, and security in the presence of slavery, fear, and despair.
Milton Ferguson, President, Midwestern Seminary

Develop a growth plan: 1. in commitment to Christ; 2. in relationships; 3. in quality church membership; 4. in maturity; 5. in witnessing and stewardship; and 6. in a disciplined reading program.
William F. Graham, Dir., Book Store Division, BSSB

Pour resources into new Convention areas for purposes such as television and radio. Do periodic mailouts from the Sunday School Board on a large scale. Make biblical, authentic, complete evangelism top priority in all training and publication.
Thomas E. Halsell, Exec. Sec., West Virginia

Southern Baptists cannot complete any assignment given the church in their own strength. They will succeed in proportion to their own commitment to the Lord revealed in Holy Scriptures as interpreted by the Holy Spirit.
Earl Kelly, Exec. Sec.-Treas., Mississippi

Let's pray for one another and "seek the old paths, wherein are the good ways." Let's be patient with one another as *God's workmanship* which has not yet received his finishing touch.
Don Moore, Exec. Dir., Arkansas

All Christians are called to serve and to minister. Each of us should consistently practice the basics of the Christian life, equip ourselves for mission beyond our own ability, and totally commit ourselves to whatever service our Lord calls us.
William M. Pinson, Jr., Exec. Dir., Texas

Look beyond your own church field. Discover the purpose and opportunity God has put within your reach.
Cecil C. Sims, Exec. Dir.-Treas., Northwest Convention

World conditions have changed unbelievably, but God and his Word have not. God will yet do great things through us and for us if we *return* to 2 Chronicles 7:14 and *stay there!*
K. Owen White, President, SBC, 1964-1965

modern era, one of which was the so-called Prayer Revival of 1858-1859. Could one person pray, and, calling others to pray, be the means by which God would ignite a spiritual awakening?

On September 23, 1857, a noon prayer meeting was called in New York City by Jeremiah C. Lampere. Lampere was a hard-working merchant turned lay missionary at the Old Dutch North Church. Only six came to pray. Nothing extraordinary at all. But within six months, ten thousand businessmen were gathering daily in at least twenty such prayer meetings across the city. In a short period of time, the spiritual awakening spread like wildfire across this nation. More than a million new converts came into the kingdom of Christ.

From the human point of view, we don't know all the whys and wherefores. We do know that God has asked us to pray. Will you? It will make a difference among our great Southern Baptist people!

A People Turning to God

Historically, spiritual awakenings have included a greater sense of personal and corporate sin, a heightened sense of the righteousness and holiness of God. Spiritual awakening is always turning from sin—returning to God.

"[If] My people . . . seek My face and turn from their wicked ways. . . ."

God calls his people to seek his face. The expression *the face of God* and related expressions are used a number of times in the Old Testament. Natural man left to his own devices would never seek the face of God. There is something in natural man that is averse to the living God. Even among his people, there is a fear of seeing the face of God. Whenever people begin seeking God, it is God's working in them.

At Sinai God had Moses warn the people not to gaze on him, lest they perish. Jacob was surprised that he saw God face to face and lived through it. The angel of the Lord told Gideon that he would not die even though he had seen God's face. Manoah, Samson's father, expressed the fear that he would die after seeing the face of God. The young Isaiah felt undone before the Lord in the Temple. Only God himself can make it safe for a human being to see his face and live. Through chastenings and purgings of fire like the seraphim in the Temple touching a burning coal to Isaiah's lips, the Lord prepares us and enables us to see his face.

I fear that we Southern Baptists have lost the sense of God's holiness and with it the awfulness of sin. We have at times been off balance in emphasizing only the positive. The negative is there, too, and we must deal with it if we are to proclaim the whole counsel of God. We're not only to be filled with the Spirit but also we are not to be drunk with wine. The gift of God *is* eternal life, but the wages of sin is still death. When we forget to deal with negatives, the positive notes are muted.

In our longing for a spiritual awakening, let us not fear to preach the whole gospel: the love *and* wrath of God; the consequences of faith *and* unbelief, or repentance *and* rebellion; salvation *and* destruction; mercy *and* judgment; heaven *and* hell. The call of the covenant God is always "turn and live." Not to turn is to die.

Turn and return to our God in the Old Testament has several powerful senses: (1) like a rebellious subject returning in obedience to a rightful sovereign, (2) like an unfaithful wife returning in unqualified trust to her wronged husband, (3) like a worshiper rejecting idols and turning to Jehovah God. Repentance brings a new way of life, mind, orientation, and direction refusing to lean on worldly help. In the New Testament, repentance expands to include a change of mind about sins that includes (1) deep sorrow for sin, grief over wronging another, even hatred of sin, and (2) a change in the direction and behavior of life.

Jesus started his public ministry with the solemn message: "repent, for the kingdom of heaven is at hand" (Matt. 4:17). As a great people of God, let a large number of us call out in broken compassion: "repent, for God's spiritual awakening and powerful breakthrough is at hand."

Our God Who Hears His People

Spiritual awakening is God's great desire for us. He wants it more than we do. He knows our condition in minute detail. He knows what we most need. So let us, as Southern Baptists, know ourselves to be God's people. Let us live out our lives and do his bidding under his providential care.

"[If] My people . . . then I will hear from heaven . . ."

Moses had fled Egypt. He was afraid that he would be killed for slaying an Egyptian whom he saw beating a Hebrew. In the land of Midian, Moses settled down, married, and worked as a shepherd. One day he was tending his father-in-law's flock on the back side of the desert near Horeb. In this very ordinary circumstance, the Lord appeared to Moses in a bush that burned but was not consumed.

The Lord revealed himself to Moses as the God of his fathers Abraham, Isaac, and Jacob. Beyond that, he identified himself as the great I AM, the self-existent One, fount of all life and blessedness.

I think it is significant that in the first part of his conversation with Moses, God used three words expressing his perception of the situation and two verbs expressing action.

> I have *seen* the affliction of my people.
> I have *heard* their cry.
> I *know* their sorrows.
> I am *come down*
> *to deliver* them.

The great I AM was aware of the slaves in Egypt. He cared that they were in bondage. And he was going to do something about it. The God of the Exodus was the God speaking to Solomon and saying, "I will hear from heaven." "From heaven" speaks of the perfect place of God's abode where he reigns with power and splendor.

This beautiful phrase *from heaven* introduces us to two encouraging truths about God: (1) he is present everywhere to hear us, and (2) he is powerful to help us, to govern the affairs of this whole universe, and to be sovereign in our lives. It has encouraged me to know that God was on mission in this world long before there was a Baptist family and that he is alongside us now. He controls and cares for his created universe and invites us to enter his work. He gives guidance in the history of humanity.

God answers prayer in his own time with a *yes, no,* or *later.* God in sovereignty created people free with the will to choose and love and obey and live, or reject and refuse and die. God's providence tolerates pain and suffering in this world, teaching us that he is here not to make life pleasant but to shape character and to make us co-workers in his kingdom. The redeeming purpose of God is demonstrated once and for all in the suffering, death, resurrection, and eternal life of his Son Jesus Christ.

The idea of God's providence is not expressed by a single Hebrew or Greek word. Rather, it is a treasured truth expressed in many ways. It is normally defined as the unceasing activity of the Creator, whereby, in overflowing bounty and goodwill (Matt. 5:45-48), he upholds his creatures in ordered existence (Acts 17:28), guides all events and circumstances (Ps. 107), and directs everything to its appointed goal, for his own glory (Eph. 1:9-12).

In the hymn "God Moves in a Mysterious Way," we sing William Cowper's words:

> God moves in a mysterious way
>   His wonders to perform;
> He plants his footsteps in the sea
>   And rides upon the storm.
> . . . .
> Behind a frowning providence
>   He hides a shining face

And Henry Ward Beecher once preached: "Everything that happens in the world is part of the great plan of God running through all time."

God hears the prayers of his people and providentially cares for them. Benjamin Franklin is quoted as saying: "The longer I live the more convincing proofs I see of this truth, that God governs in the affairs of men, and if a sparrow cannot fall to the ground without his notice, is it probable that our empire can rise without his aid?"

To paraphrase, Is it possible that the denomination of Southern Baptists can rise and stand without his aid? No—not at all! Therefore, there is this longing for a spiritual awakening in our midst.

One of the greatest experiences a person can have is to be heard—for someone to really listen. How much more so to be heard by the living God! Knowing that we are heard and known thoroughly by the Lord will make a great difference in our lives.

One of our own Baptist hymn writers, B. B. McKinney, knew this truth and expressed it so well in "Have Faith In God."

In the first three stanzas, notice the verbs that speak of God's perception of us. In the final verse, there is the emphasis on God's power and his desire to act on our behalf.

> *He sees and knows* all the way you have trod.
> Your earnest plea he will *never forget.*
> His heart *is touched* with your grief and despair.
> He *provides* for his own.
> He *cannot fail.*
> He *rules.*
> He *reigns.*

God hears from heaven. That is enough.

Our God Forgiving His People

Hearing us as he does, God knows that our greatest need is to be forgiven. Great spiritual power is generated in the experience of being forgiven. A forgiven people is a people ready for God's mission.

"[If] My people, . . . I . . . will forgive their sin and will heal their land."

The Hebrew word for "forgive" used here is used only in connection with God. God's forgiveness of human beings is qualitatively different from human forgiveness. Human beings' forgiveness of each other is limited and provisional. "I will forgive you if . . ." God's forgiveness is unlimited but it has to be received with a heart set on returning to God and walking in God's ways.

Forgiveness, whether human or divine, is always costly. It costs to forgive. There is a nagging sense in all human beings that sin must be paid for. All kinds of strange practices have been the result of people trying to pay for their own sin. But we need not do so and indeed cannot pay for our sins. God himself has paid. In his Son, Jesus Christ, he has taken away the sin of the world. This redemptive theme runs through both the Old and New Testaments. When the angel of the Lord appeared to Joseph in a dream, he instructed him to name Mary's child *Jesus,* "For it is He who will save His people from their sins" (Matt. 1:21).

To be forgiven assumes that the person recognizes the need for forgiveness. In our Southern Baptist tradition, we seem to have mental checklists of certain sins. If we don't do any of those, we feel that we've overcome sin and don't have any need to be forgiven.

We don't have to read far in the Gospels and the rest of the New Testament to see that sin is a broader and deeper understanding than what we have on our checklist. If we don't feel the need to be forgiven, it is probably because we are blind to our sin. The person who is unaware of personal sin quite often sees that sin in another person. He condemns the other person for the sin that he himself is guilty of. Paul recognized this in Romans 2. In the Sermon on the Mount, Jesus commanded us to take the big logs out of our own eyes before we try to help a neighbor remove a speck from his eye.

Once we recognize our sin, we need only bring it to God.

Accepting forgiveness is the free choice of individuals by faith and repentance, based on what Jesus has done for us.

A person who is forgiven will renounce the old life, turning from self and the world to God. A person who experiences forgiveness overflows with gratitude to God. He is ready to leave old purposes to follow the will of God. Isaac Watts expressed this experience of forgiving love mediated through the crucified Christ when he exclaimed, in "When I Survey the Wondrous Cross":

> Love so amazing, so divine,
> Demands my soul, my life, my all.

Being forgiven leads us to forgive those who have wronged us. Where we feel unforgiveness toward another person, we might begin looking for the reason by asking the Lord to show us some areas in our own lives that need forgiveness.

When we experience God's forgiveness, we have the desire to make right, where possible, those things that we have done to harm other persons. When my son, Philip, was four years old, he was playing with my tape recorder. In the process of doing so, he broke it. He did not try to hide it but came to me, telling me what he had done and asking for my forgiveness. I forgave him. But the story didn't end there. Several days later I discovered that Phil brought a catalog to his mother so she could help him order a tape recorder to replace the one he had broken. He didn't have to do it. But, being forgiven, he wanted to. There is no telling what we could do for the Lord if we felt forgiven and let that sense of being forgiven lead us to forgive others and to make amendments and restitution where we have wronged others.

May we not let this longing for spiritual awakening die out in us. Let us nourish it and let it grow. Let us hear God's Word, his promise to Solomon, "[If] My people who are called by My name [will] . . . I will . . ."

I have great hope and expectation for us as a Southern Baptist people.

We need to hear this promise, really hear it—not just with our heads but deeper and deeper in our hearts.

We will be the people God wants us to be, not a church on life's traffic circle without a sense of direction or mission, not a church saved by legalism or doctrine or good works. We will be the people of God, not a church under the flagwaving national religion as the way out.

We will be the people of God, not a church on Madison Avenue buying the sophistication and appearance of worldly ways and things.

We will be the people of God, not a church on Lake Placid paddling the canoe of peace at any price.

We will be the people of God, not a church on Main Street, U.S.A., being nice to everybody about everything just because they are sincere.

We will be the people of God, not a church at the county fair just along for the ride and fun of it.

We will be the people of God, not a church in the back alley enjoying the pleasure of sin for a season, not a church by the fountain of youth searching for every passing fad to make us young again, not a church of yesterday that refuses to believe God's promise of forgiveness and power for his people. By God's grace and goodness, we will, as Southern Baptists, be a people of God.

Notes

1. *Annual of the Southern Baptist Convention,* 1906, p. 40.

5
Servant
Leadership

Challenge #5: As a people of God, let us acknowledge, develop, practice, and follow servant leadership patterned after the self-giving service of our Lord both within the local churches and throughout the denominational network.

Mark 10:43-45: But it is not so among you, but whoever wishes to become great among you shall be your servant: and whoever wishes to be first among you shall be slave of all. For even the Son of Man did not come to be served, but to serve, and to give His life a ransom for many.

Painting the Dream: Someone in the church must paint the dream. . . . For anything great to happen there must be a great dream. The growing edge church will be a painter of great dreams for *all* of its people, something to lift their sights above the ordinary and give them a great goal to strive for—something for each person to strive for.

ROBERT K. GREENLEAF[1]

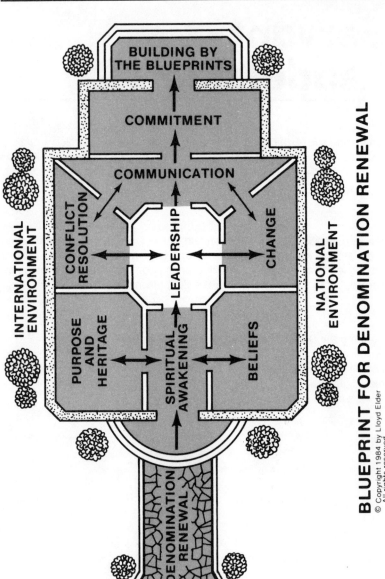

BUILDING BY
THE BLUEPRINTS

COMMITMENT

COMMUNICATION

CONFLICT
RESOLUTION

LEADERSHIP

CHANGE

INTERNATIONAL
ENVIRONMENT

NATIONAL
ENVIRONMENT

PURPOSE
AND
HERITAGE

SPIRITUAL
AWAKENING

BELIEFS

DENOMINATION
RENEWAL

BLUEPRINT FOR DENOMINATION RENEWAL

Leadership based on spiritual awakening is at the very center of our blueprint for denomination renewal. We will have leaders for tomorrow. We always have. But the well-being of our denomination and its future depend on the kinds of persons who serve as leaders.

The bedrock conviction on which this chapter is built is that Jesus Christ is our supreme model of a Christian leader. We who lead God's people should continually look to Jesus so that in all aspects of our lives—including our pattern of leading—we are following his example.

In the present chapter I draw on studies of leadership by behavioral and management experts. I have found that these disciplines can give us considerable insight into various styles of leadership, some of which *we would not want to practice.* However, they can help us see a lot about our own way of leading—good or bad. But theory is not enough. Our most important lessons about leadership often come from leaders we have seen and known.

Down through the years I have known a few outstanding Baptist leaders. Some of them are well known to the denomination; others are just as great but known only to a few of us. I have worked with these leaders, walked in their paths, drawn from their strength, shared their tears and sorrows, observed their limitations, learned from their wisdom, and thrilled at their devotion to Christ and to Baptist causes.

Most of my experiences with Baptist leaders have been beneficial and productive. Although there may be a leadership crisis in many areas of our world and some places among Southern Baptists, by and large we have been blessed of God with able and gifted leaders. I am deeply grateful to God for what has been and what is now the basis for renewal within our denomination. I do not call us from wrong to right, not even from good to better. Rather, the challenge to servant leadership is cast into the context, process, and hope for denomination renewal.

The development and renewal of leadership are essential to

the renewal and effectiveness of any organization. Let's begin by looking at several definitions of leadership.

Dalton E. McFarland defines leadership as "the ability of an individual to influence others to work beyond ordinary levels to achieve goals."[2]

Paul Hersey and Kenneth H. Blanchard characterize leadership as "the process of influencing the activities of an individual or group in efforts toward a goal achievement in a given situation."[3]

James J. Cribbins defines leadership as "the ability to gain consensus and commitment to common objectives, beyond organizational requirements, which are attained with the experience of contribution and satisfaction on the part of the work group."[4]

> Leadership over human beings is exercised when persons with certain motives and purposes mobilize, in competition or conflict with others, institutional, political, psychological, and other resources so as to arouse, engage, and satisfy the motives of followers. This is done in order to realize goals mutually held by both leaders and followers. . . . All leaders are actual or potential power holders, but not all power holders are leaders.[5]

There are some common threads running through these different definitions. Leadership is someone influencing someone else to achieve a goal.

There are many ways people influence each other, ranging from physical coercion to *agape* love. Moreover, there are many goals to be achieved, ranging from the most harmful and destructive to the most creative and beneficial.

Baptist Leadership Network

The Southern Baptist denomination is not one large organization guided by a single leader. Rather, it is a complex network of large and small diverse organizations made up of people. If we are to experience renewal within this large and complex network, it is imperative that we do the following things:

1. Understand the decentralized nature, the overlapping network, and the diversity of Baptist leadership;

2. Call upon each Baptist leader to function within his or her legitimate area of responsibility;
3. Urge each Baptist leader to contribute to genuine denomination renewal at the personal and organizational level;
4. Encourage each leader to exercise authority, power, and position in a way that is consistent with New Testament servant leadership.

Now, let's look at a thumbnail sketch of our Baptist leadership network. This should point out the complexity of the leadership roles and possible sources of conflict. This should also make us aware of the potential for good should there be renewal within the denominational leadership team.

Local Church Authority

Within the Southern Baptist denomination, the most basic source of authority is the local congregation. The local church is the foundation for all other authority and leadership. In fact, the local church has been rightly called "Baptist headquarters."

What factors combine to give our 36,000 churches such a leadership role? Consider these:

- the lordship of Christ alone over his church;
- the Great Commission to the church;
- the autonomy and democratic polity of the local church;
- the local church's voluntary cooperation with other churches and Baptist bodies;
- the local church's election of messengers, not delegates,[6] to other Baptist bodies;
- the local church's voluntary financial support of denominational programs and institutions;
- the local church's voluntary utilization of denominational materials and services; and
- the local church's freedom to follow or not follow other leaders within the denominational family.

It is in the local church that most Baptist laypersons and many pastors have their greatest leadership impact.

Baptist churches have historically cherished and maintained a healthy balance of authority based on the principles of independence and interdependence. The renewal of the local church and its disciplined exercise of authority is foundational to leadership renewal in the denomination.

Elected Leadership

Church messengers to other Baptist bodies elect officers to serve in voluntary places of leadership: moderators of associations, presidents of state conventions, and the officers of the Southern Baptist Convention.

These officers serve briefly, usually one or two years, and primarily have presiding and committee appointment responsibilities. However, in recent years, Southern Baptist Convention presidents, claiming Baptist grass-roots support, have had an enlarged public influence on the direction of the denomination.

The office of president and its powers of appointment have become the focus of leadership control in the Southern Baptist Convention. Perhaps too many Southern Baptists have lost sight of the fact that the seat of Baptist authority is in the local church. That is where the denominational power resides, where the work is done, and where the health and effectiveness of the denomination is ultimately measured. Elected leadership that serves the best interest of the local churches serves the denomination well.

Trustee Leadership

Since the denomination is a network of autonomous bodies involving fourteen million Baptists, trusteeship is at the heart of the actual functioning of the denomination's vast work. Boards, commissions, agencies, and institutions are held in trust and legal ownership by the boards of trustees, directors, and commissioners. These boards, composed of ordained and laypersons, are elected by Baptist bodies and held accountable for overseeing the purpose, policies, administration, and performance of these entities.

Trustees normally serve from six to eight years. They provide continuity of leadership, stability of administration, integrity of purpose, and diversity of representation.

In the present era there is a heightened sense of interest in Baptist trustees. From my viewpoint, this is a good thing for several reasons:

- The trustee is not merely a position of honor but of responsibility.
- The trustee does indeed have legal and denominational accountability for the institution or agency.
- The trustee is concerned with bylaws and policies of the institution, delegating administration of the institution to elected administrative officers.
- The trustee should be able to discern between unrealistic popular expectations and demands made of an institution and its legitimate obligation to those it serves.
- The trustee is by definition obligated to be a supporter, not an inside guard or critic.

My experience through the years has been that Baptists have knowledgeable, capable, and dedicated trustees serving their institutions.

Let the recent attention given this leadership role sharpen our intention to elect skilled, devout, denominationally committed Baptists to fill these significant leadership roles.

Executive Leadership

Baptist entities which are responsible to the Southern Baptist Convention and the state Baptist conventions are usually guided by an executive officer. Each officer, by whatever title, is elected by an authorized board and is delegated the responsibility of administration within approved bylaws and policies.

The officer is held accountable on behalf of Baptists to fulfill the purpose of the agency or institution and quite often to do so in keeping with a prescribed doctrinal statement such as *The Baptist Faith and Message* of 1963.

An executive leader often (1) functions as part of the denomination's leadership, (2) coordinates with other Baptist bodies, (3) responds to external pressures and expectations, (4) integrates internal diversity and agendas, (5) operates on inadequate resources, and (6) pleads for the loyalty and support of Baptists who own the institution he or she administers.

Southern Baptists have every right to expect and receive from executive leaders competent and faithful leadership in the mainstream of Baptist constituency.

Program Leadership

In addition to executive leadership, certain agencies and programs have leaders who exert major impact on the denomination and its churches. These include Sunday School, Church Training, Church Music, Woman's Missionary Union, and Baptist Brotherhood.

These and other leaders, through program materials and services, shape the work, spirit, character, and direction of the entire Baptist family.

Baptist associational leadership has a crucial role as it provides a variety of program needs within the context of the local churches. One of the celebrated strengths of Baptist life and growth continues to be strong, able program leadership.

Editorial Leadership

Communication is the lifeblood in any organization or network of organizations that seek to work together. Historically, the power of communication has been in the pen, and it will continue to be so. In addition, the emerging electronic media will have significant potential for influencing Southern Baptists.

Baptist Press and the state Baptist papers have a leadership role expressed through (1) freedom of the press, (2) editorial statements on key issues, (3) news coverage of Baptist events, (4) selecting what information will be communicated and what events covered, (5) image making of Baptist personalities, (6) promotion of Baptist programs and efforts, (7) direct access to the homes of Southern Baptist families, and (8) relationship to the public media.

Editors have often been praised as courageous prophets, as well as criticized as part of the establishment among Southern Baptists. In my estimate, the two new Southern Baptist telecommunications efforts will complement and extend this editorial leadership role: American Christian Television System (ACTS) in the public media and Baptist Telecommunication Network (BTN) in the local church communications system.

Pastoral Leadership

The pastors of local churches have historically wielded a vital leadership role not only in their own congregations but often within the denomination. They have done this through the pulpit, as well as other communications media.

For good or bad, pastors and other church staff members are those most often elected to denominational places of responsibility. They make up the majority of messengers at any Southern Baptist Convention. What the minister says and does continues to have a pacesetting effect on Baptist laypersons. The pastor's skill and spirit in the area of communication is important in a time of communication crises.

Lay Leadership

As a rule, Baptist laypersons have their greatest leadership role in the local church. There is a growing emphasis today on recovering the gifts and ministry of laypersons. Many boards and committees include lay membership, but few involve significant laywomen participation. Great concern has been expressed by many that not enough laypersons have been called to serve in major denominational leadership posts.

The mobilization of the laity is absolutely imperative if Bold

Mission Thrust is to be a reality. The equipping of Baptist laypersons for Christian leadership throughout the layers and levels of our society is an awesome challenge for our churches and denomination.

Informal Leadership

Within our denomination, as within any large organization, there is a formal (official) and an informal (unofficial) leadership system. Informal leaders often shape the environment and context in which Southern Baptists do their work. They do so in the following roles: (1) speakers who become popular throughout the Convention and conference circuits; (2) officers of pastors' conferences and other such groups; (3) pastors of large churches who are newsmakers; (4) Baptist laypersons in significant public posts, such as ex-President Jimmy Carter; (5) caucus leaders for certain doctrinal or political positions; (6) experts who research, speak, and publish within their recognized fields; and (7) those who work in structures which are adjacent to but not part of denominational institutions.

It is difficult to assess the number or impact of these informal leaders. Only Southern Baptists themselves who choose to be led can determine whether such informal leaders will strengthen the denomination or contribute to its fragmentation.

Institutional Leadership

Most Baptists recognize that from time to time a particular Baptist institution rises to an important leadership role. This is true not because of the contribution of a single leader but because of consistent and conspicuous leadership of the total organization.

We know both from Baptist history and from personal experience of at least six or seven times in our history when our institutions have risen to important leadership roles at crucial times. Therefore, it is most appropriate for Southern Baptists to carefully measure the contribution and direction of their institutions.

Leadership Styles

We have considered the *kinds* of leadership and authority evident among Southern Baptists. Now let's look at several *styles* of leadership that would be found not only among Southern Baptists but in any human situation where leaders emerge.

Leadership and leadership style have been the object of considerable study in recent decades. Leadership styles can be characterized in many different ways. One of the most helpful is The Managerial Grid® developed by Robert R. Blake and Jane S. Mouton.

The Managerial Grid®[7] (see next page) gives a visual representation of five basic styles of management. Of course, there are far more than five management styles, but these five are sufficient to show the various combinations of attitudes that managers might have toward (1) productivity—the extent to which the purpose of the organization is achieved, (2) the people in the organization, and (3) the use of power and authority in getting the work done.

Impoverished Management Style (1,1)

This style of management has sometimes been called "caretaker administration," "bankrupt leadership," or having a nonleader in a leadership role. A (1,1) manager has little concern for productivity *or* for people in the organization. Such a person shows little involvement with people and exercises little power or authority.

This leader's motto is, "I will do just enough to get by." Such a person desires little, strives for little, gives little, gets little, and cares little one way or another.

Fear is the primary motivator for such a manager. He may fear being abandoned and have a need to hang on. Such a person may become a defeated hermit, withdrawing from people and action. His attitude may be contagious in the organization, or it may provoke an aggressive reaction on the part of others.

Figure 5-1. The Managerial Grid®

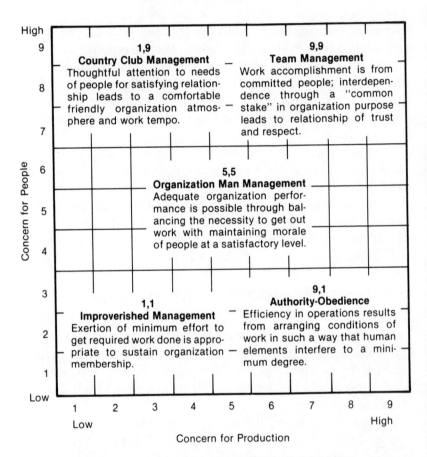

The Managerial Grid ® figure from *The New Managerial Grid*, by Robert R. Blake and Jane Srygley Mouton. Houston: Gulf Publishing Company, Copyright © 1978, page 11. Reproduced by permission.

Authority-Obedience Style (9,1)

This leader has an unusually high concern for productivity and achievement of goals but low concern for people in the organization. This type of manager works in such a way that the human element interferes to a minimal degree in his going after results.

A (9,1) leader exercises power in a unilateral way. The attitude of such a leader is, "I will influence you, but you will influence me little if at all."

Leaders of this style are often described as driving, autocratic, taskmasters, dictators, and authoritarian. Such leaders believe that most people have to be driven rather than led. They have a strong need for control, mastery, and domination. Follower response is often adverse, if not antagonistic, toward this type of leader and the organization.

Country Club Style (1,9)

This leader provides a compatible and pleasant administration. He has low concern for performance but high concern for people. This kind of leader believes thoughtful attention to the needs of people leads to a comfortable, friendly organizational atmosphere and smooth-working tempo. This laissez-faire leader believes that when people are happy, the objectives of the organization will be reached with no need for guidance. Such a leader prides himself on being a people person and likes to see the organization as one big happy family.

A (1,9) leader is motivated primarily out of fear of rejection. He has a high need for warmth and approval. Some followers enjoy this style. Others will seek ways to make a larger contribution than is possible under such leadership.

Organization Man Style (5,5)

The (5,5) manager has a moderate concern for both performance and people. His is a "constituency-centered" administration. Adequate organization performance is possible through balancing concern for results with a concern for the morale of people. The (5,5) leader often "goes along to get along" with the majority, hoping to avoid being seen as unreasonable. He seeks to avoid actions that might upset the applecart and lead to criticism. His aim is to be average—satisfactory to everybody. This organization man may appear as a compromiser, a defender of the status quo, a benevolent dictator, and, at times, a democratic leader.

His primary motivators are the fear of being embarrassed and the desire to be "in," to be popular. Those who follow such a leader sense they can get by with only average, appropriate efforts. Conformity is expected and rewarded.

Team Management Style (9,9)

This leader integrates a high concern for organization performance with a high concern for people. He tends to believe that most people have the motivation to achieve and don't have to be driven to do so. The (9,9) leader believes that when people see themselves as having a common stake in the organization and its goals, they will work together with a high degree of respect and trust.

This goal-oriented team leader acts often in the role of coach, equipper, and encourager. The (9,9) leader can be analytical or expressive as the situation requires. Such a leader is motivated by the fear of betraying a trust and a desire for fulfillment through making a contribution.

There are other schemes that might be used to characterize leaders. Tables 5-1 and 5-2 show other ways of categorizing leaders and leadership styles. In our own history and life as Southern Baptists, we have had all kinds of leadership. Following are some descriptive phrases that might be used of some of our leaders:

- champion of a cause,
- exemplar of a movement,
- hero of an epoch,
- defender of a position,
- statesman calling us to the high road,
- visionary moving us forward,

- teacher developing our minds,
- prophets speaking with certainty,
- maverick threatening the status quo,
- advocate of those without station, and
- expert exercising authority.

There are two points worth making about leadership roles and styles. First, they are overlapping and not mutually exclusive. Second, in various situations different leadership styles and roles may be appropriate or effective.

Our experience of renewal in our denomination will depend on those who are leaders—not just leaders who have some position but all those whom God uses to influence others in kingdom work. Those whom God most uses will be servant leaders. In order to consider this concept more fully, let's look at servant leadership in the New Testament.

Servant Leadership: A New Testament Pattern

Servant leadership was not only taught by Jesus but also found its perfect expression in him. Consider the request of his disciples, James and John, that they be given a favored place in his kingdom. Their request is reported in Mark 10:35-45. I see six fundamental truths in this text.

1. Followers of Jesus, like other human beings, have ambitions (v. 35-37). James and John, Zebedee's sons, did a good thing in bringing their ambition to Jesus. God wants us to bring all of ourselves to him. If we try to hide our ambition from ourselves, others, or God, we block the work of God in our lives.

But James and John weren't just a little ambitious. They had towering ambitions. They wanted Jesus to give them a blank check! In his wisdom, Jesus pressed them to be more specific. They responded by saying all they wanted was to be first in Christ's kingdom—to share his glory, to sit on his right hand and left hand, that's all!

Ambition isn't a new thing. It's as old as Adam and as new as the morning newspaper. Ambition for leadership is found among

TABLE 5-1. Leaders who are merely successful.

Executive	Motto	Characteristics	Typical Behavior
Bureaucrat	"We go by the book."	Rational, formal, impersonal, politely proper, disciplined. May be slow-moving and/or jealous of his or her function, rights, and prerogatives. Well versed in the organizational "rocks and shoals."	Follows the letter of the law. Stickler for rules and procedures. Task-oriented, less concerned with people. Logical strategist but may be politically astute and/or a nitpicker.
Zealot	"We do things my way, in spite of the organization."	A loner. Impatient, outspoken, overly independent, extremely competent. Jumps the traces, a nuisance to the bureaucrats. Insensitive to the feelings of others. Modest political skills. Fair but demanding.	Devoted to the good of the organization, *as he or she sees it.* Excessively task-oriented but has little concern for people. Aggressive and domineering. Is insistent but fiercely supports all who are on his or her side.
Machiavellian	"We depersonalize and use you."	Self-oriented, shrewd, devious, calculating, amoral, manipulative. Excellent insight into people's weaknesses. Extremely opportunistic. Flexible, ranges from seeming collaboration to pitiless aggression. Cold but can be charming.	Treats people as things to be exploited and outwitted. Cooperates only when it is to his or her advantage. Personal considerations do not enter into thinking. Must win at any price and in any way possible.
Missionary	"We love one another."	Much too concerned with people and what they think of him or her. Subjective in orientation. Likable but tries too hard to be liked. Excellent interpersonal skills but does not win respect. Insists that conflict and friction be smoothed over.	A soft manager who prizes harmony above all else. Low task orientation. Gets emotionally involved. Acts on a personal basis. Tends to do what is popular or will make him or her liked. Inclined to ignore harder organizational requirements.

Climber	"I vault over anyone I can."	Striving, driving, energetic, self-oriented. Often smooth and polished but always aggressive. Usually opportunistic, always plotting next move or maneuver. No loyalty to the organization or to anyone in it. Often quite competent. Constantly fronts self.	High political skills. Excellent at maneuvering into the limelight. Predatory toward weaker managers. Welcomes and initiates self-propelling change. May have high task orientation but for self-serving purposes, not for the good of the firm. Adroit with people but has no interest in them.
Exploiter	"When I bark, they jump."	Arrogant, insistent, abusive. Demeaning, coercive, vindictive, domineering. Often quite competent. Rigid, prejudiced, given to snap judgments. Exploits others' weaknesses.	Exerts constrictive and personal controls. Flogs anyone who is vulnerable. Uses pressure and fear to get things done. Demands subservience. High task orientation. Sees people as minions.
Temporizer	"We bend to the strongest pressure."	Procrastinating, compromising, vacillating. Earns contempt. Feels a helpless sense of being put upon. Survival instincts may be superior. May be politically aware.	Low task orientation, low people concern. Reacts to the strongest immediate pressure. Reactive, not active. Behavior varies with pressures.
Glad-Hander	"We sell the sizzle, not the steak."	Ebullient, superficial, effusive, deceptively friendly, extroverted. Excellent interpersonal skills. Lacks depth, minimally competent. May be an excellent politician. Survival instincts superior. Talkative, humorous, lacks substance.	Sells himself or herself very well. Low or modest task orientation. Unconcerned with people but excellent in dealing with them. Gets by on "personality." Always seeks to impress and to improve his or her position. May use people but rarely threatens them.

Reprinted, by permission of the publisher, from LEADERSHIP: STRATEGIES FOR ORGANIZATIONAL EFFECTIVENESS by James J. Cribbin, pp. 36–37, © 1981 by AMACON, a division of American Management Associations, New York. All rights reserved.

TABLE 5-2. Leaders who are effective.

Executive	Motto	Characteristics	Typical Behavior
Entrepreneur	"We do it my way. Only risk-taking achievers need apply."	Extremely competent, forceful, individualistic, egocentric, dominant, self-confident. Extraordinary achievement drive. Innovative, very firm-minded and strong-willed. Something of a loner. Not only listens to his or her own drummer but composes his or her own music. Can be very loyal, protective, and generous to team.	Unable to work well in a subordinate position for very long. Must be prime mover and binds small team to him or her with great loyalty. Offers challenges, opportunities to succeed, and great returns on risks taken. Does not develop subordinates. Is not open to ideas that differ from his or her own. Gets involved in all aspects of the organization. Exercises very tight control. Motivates by example, rewards, and fear.
Corporateur	"I call the shots, but we all work together on my team."	Dominant but not domineering. Quite directive but gives people considerable freedom. Consultative but not really participative. Sizes up people well but relates to them on a surface level. Cordial to people but keeps them at arm's length.	Concerned about the good of the organization. Wins respect. High task orientation. Polished and professional manager. Makes people feel needed. Delegates and consults but keeps effective control. Supportive but not emotionally involved with subordinates.
Developer	"People are our most important resource."	Trustful of subordinates. Intent on helping them actualize their potential. Excellent human relations skills. Wins personal loyalty, builds a supportive and achieving climate. Fine coach and counselor.	Very high people orientation. Although productivity is superior, at times people considerations may take precedence. People feel needed. Delegates and consults but keeps effective control. Supportive and emotionally involved with subordinates.

Type	Motto	Traits	Behavior
Craftsman	"We do important work as perfectly as we can."	Amiable, conservative, extremely conscientious. Principled, very knowledgeable and skilled, self-reliant. Highly task-oriented. Proud of competence. Work- and family-oriented. Self-contented, honest, straightforward, perfectionistic, independent, analytical, mild-mannered.	Likes to innovate, build, and tinker with quality products. Not overly concerned with status or politics. Motivated by a desire for excellence. Self-demanding but supportive of subordinates. Competes with projects, not people. Restive with organizational red tape. Likes to solve problems alone or in a small group.
Integrator	"We build consensus and commitment."	Egalitarian, supportive, participative. Excellent interpersonal skills. Superior people insight. A team builder, catalyst, adept at unifying different inputs. A subtle leader, prefers group decision making.	Shares the leadership. Thinks in terms of associates rather than subordinates. Gives great freedom and authority. Welcomes the ideas of others. Geared to win-win interaction. Acts as a synergistic catalyst.
Gamesman	"We win together, but I must win more than you."	Fast-moving, flexible, upwardly mobile. Very knowledgeable and skilled. Autonomous, risk-taking, assertive, and intent on winning but not petty or vindictive. Innovative. Takes no great pleasure in another's loss or defeat. Opportunistic but not unethical. Not depressed by defeat.	Wants to be respected as a strategist who builds a winning team. Enjoys the game of winning within the organization's rules. Enjoys competition, jockeying, and maneuvering. Sharp, skilled, unbiased, and tough manager who challenges and rewards contribution. Impersonally eliminates the weak and nonachievers.

Reprinted, by permission of the publisher, from LEADERSHIP: STRATEGIES FOR ORGANIZATIONAL EFFECTIVENESS by James J. Cribbin, pp. 44-45, © 1981 by AMACON, a division of American Management Associations, New York. All rights reserved.

Baptists just as it was in Jesus' inner circle. We cannot rid ourselves of ambition. We do well to follow the example of James and John in bringing our ambitions to Jesus.

2. Jesus tested their ambitions by his own standards (vv. 38-40). These two disciples wanted an exalted title, a place of prominence, glory, and high leadership. But Jesus wanted them, as he wants us, to get down to the reality of the Christian life: "Are you able to drink the cup that I drink, or to be baptized with the baptism with which I am baptized?" (v. 38). He was asking, Are you able to live my life, walk my road, die my death?

They replied, "We are able" (v. 39).

Jesus didn't give James and John their request. Nor does he grant upon demand our requests for leadership and honor today. His primary gift is his own kind of life. Places of honor in his kingdom are given by kingdom principles. As twentieth-century disciples, so much captured by the standards and expectations of the world, don't we have much to learn from this acid test of Christ?

3. Ambitions often create a divisive spirit of criticism (v. 41). The ten disciples became righteously indignant at the request of the two brothers. Why? It is likely that the anger of the ten was ignited because they, also, had ambition. James and John had simply moved faster in making their request. As it did in Jesus' day, ambition today creates criticism, divisiveness, and party spirit.

It is so tempting to say: I want. I want!
- I want to be first in the kingdom.
- I want to have my place in the sun.
- I want to stand in the spotlight.
- I want to be chosen for office.
- I want to be recognized as successful.
- I want to be number one, to be in charge.
- I want to make my mark in the world.
- I want to be happy and content.
- I want to be rich and famous.

Whatever our ambitions, let us bring them to Christ, openly, honestly, even in the face of criticism from others. But we dare not stop there.

4. The world has its own standards of greatness and leadership (v. 42). Jesus did not simply condemn the two brothers for their ambition nor even the ten disciples for their critical spirit. He used the occasion to contrast his own standard of greatness with that of the world: "Rulers . . . lord it over [others]; . . . great men exercise authority."

God himself has planted within each of us the desire to be somebody. After the fall, this will to be somebody was distorted. Not only do we will to be somebody but also we will to be somebody at the expense of others. Related to this is the temptation to be like God. Apart from grace, this is precisely how we are.

But there is grace. We are no longer bound to follow the world's ways. Jesus told his disciples, "It is not so among you."

5. Servant leadership is the standard of greatness among Jesus' disciples (vv. 43-44). James and John asked for glory; Jesus taught them about true greatness. They asked for prominent seats; Jesus pointed them to the priority of service. The ten disciples claimed their rights as indignant critics; Jesus told them their responsibility was to be unselfish servants. Self-giving service after the pattern of Jesus is the true course of leadership and the standard for greatness.

By this definition, every follower of Jesus is called to leadership. Greatness through service is the reward of every child of God, not just a select few.

There are a host of such Baptist leaders throughout this great denomination. These servant leaders can make a startling difference in the midst of our wounded, hurting world. The denomination permeated by such leadership will indeed experience renewal and effective kingdom service.

6. Jesus Christ himself is the perfect example of servant leadership (v. 45). During the years of his ministry, Jesus was always serving the poor, the hungry, the broken, the ill, the bereaved, the

accused, the wayward, the sinful. He came to give his life a ransom for many, bringing life-changing redemption for those who believe.

By his servant leadership, Jesus has changed the course of humanity. He towers over every other leader among people. He is the standard by which each Southern Baptist should measure his or her claim to and practice of leadership.

Servant Leadership: A Management Model

Servant leadership as taught by and exemplified in the life of Jesus is a lofty ideal. Even though Jesus' teaching is a high ideal, it is realistic to use such an ideal in our search for leadership renewal within the complexity of our denomination. This ideal is demonstrated in the best of management practice in many areas of organizational life. The ideal of servant leadership has recently been presented by Robert K. Greenleaf, a recognized authority in the field of business management. His understanding of contemporary institutions and leadership needs is evidence that servant leadership is possible and desirable in an institutional setting in our time.

Robert Greenleaf's ideal of servant leadership came to him in his last year of college. One of his professors pointed out in a lecture that the United States was becoming a nation of large institutions. The professor said that the hope for the future lay in the possibility that there were people who would lead these institutions *to perform for the public good.*

This insight had a transforming effect on the direction of Greenleaf's life. This ideal, though not stated in biblical language, is highly consistent with Jesus' teaching about servant leadership. Let me summarize some of Greenleaf's understandings from *Servant Leadership.*

1. *The servant thesis.* More servants should emerge as leaders or should follow only servant leaders.

A new moral principle is emerging which holds that the only authority deserving one's allegiance is that which is freely and knowingly granted by the led to the leader in response to, and in proportion to, the clearly evident servant stature of the leader. Those who choose to follow this principle will not casually accept the authority of existing institutions. *Rather, they will freely respond only to individuals who are chosen as leaders because they are proven and trusted as servants.* To the extent that this principle prevails in the future, the only truly viable institutions will be those that are predominantly servant-led.[8]

2. *The servant-leader.* The servant-leader is servant first. The servant-leader's primary motivation is the desire to serve. A conscious choice brings one to aspire to leadership. On the other hand, the "*leader* first" is a completely different type. Augustine recognized this difference when he concluded a passage on leadership, "So he who loves to govern rather than to do good is no bishop."

The difference between the two kinds of leaders is seen primarily in the effect of their leadership on those who are led. Under servant leadership people become healthier, wiser, freer, more autonomous, more likely to become servants themselves.

3. *Servant leadership characteristics.* Servant leadership is strong, ethical leadership in an age of antileaders. Such a leader seeks to build servant institutions in an anti-institutional era. Such leaders must be characterized by:

- listening and understanding,
- communication and imagination,
- withdrawal and reflection,
- acceptance and empathy,
- intellectual intuition,
- foresight and faith,
- awareness and perception,
- persuasion in a one-on-one situation,
- performance of one action at a time,
- conceptualizing,
- creative response,
- healing and serving,

- trustee leadership,
- power and authority, and
- personal magnetism.

The enemy of servant institutions is not the critic on the outside but the strong natural servants who have the potential to lead but do not lead or who choose to follow a nonservant leader.

4. *Institutional reconstruction.* Caring for persons, the more able and the less able serving each other, is the rock upon which a good society is built. Until recently caring was largely person-to-person. Now much of it is mediated through institutions—often large, complex, powerful, impersonal; not always competent; sometimes corrupt.

If we are to build a better society—one that is more just and loving, one that provides greater creative opportunity for its people—then servant leaders must emerge and raise the capacity of others to serve. They must do this by tapping the regenerative forces operating within the institutions of our time.

The prime force for achievement through service in any large institution is a senior administrative group committed to servant leadership. Within that group there must be an optimal balance between managers who run the day-to-day operations of the institution toward its objectives and conceptualizers who go out ahead to show the way.

5. *Servant trusteeship.* The trustees of an institution hold the legal, absolute power to manage its affairs. By accepting the servant role, trustees have the responsibility to make the institution a servant institution. This requires trust building *within* and *for* the institution. Trustees must care enough to know and know enough to care for the well-being of the institution. Trustees are in a position to have a significant impact on an institution by:

- shaping its purpose, character, programs, policies, major strategies, and goals;
- establishing the structure of the institution and selecting its administrative officers;
- maintaining ultimate authority but delegating administrative

leadership to the president and others elected to serve; and
- assessing the performance of the institution in achieving its stated goals.

Servant trusteeship will insist that the outcome of the institution's operation must be that the people who are served and those who serve will grow and become more productive.

6. *Servant leadership in the church.* The churches, like other contemporary institutions, are under pressures and influences. By worldly standards, churches are often judged to be inadequate. In some ways, churches may be judged more harshly than other institutions because the churches' role could be so pivotal in the redemption of what many regard as a sick society. In addition, the churches are often not critical enough of their actual performance and contribution because their cause is so noble.

The churches which once gave security and hope continue to function this way even though many persons, including faithful church attenders, now seek their values in their own experience. As a consequence, the alienated have multiplied for want of sufficient value-shaping influence that once was the churches' major role. The large human resources of the churches seem to be groping for a better way to serve.

The dynamics of servant leadership—the vision, the values, the staying power—are essentially religious and should become the central mission of the churches. The churches should add to their historic mission of caring for persons the mission of caring for institutions—specific institutions.

Trust must come first. This is not trust generated by leadership charisma. The only sound basis for trust is for people to have the solid experience of being served by their institutions.

Characteristics of Leadership Renewal

In this chapter I've tried to examine the leadership network of Southern Baptists, the basic leadership styles being used, the New Testament pattern of leadership for all believers, and a servant-leader model for management.

Now, let me try to summarize the leadership renewal process. Leadership renewal and development include:

1. assessment of the present climate and situation of the denomination, its leadership, and its performance;
2. awareness of the basic choices concerning patterns of leadership;
3. knowledge of the nature and process of servant leadership;
4. commitment to servant leadership, both as an ideal and as practiced in every leadership role and function; and
5. trust building among others in denominational leadership so that there is a high degree of teamwork throughout the Southern Baptist family of churches, conventions, associations, agencies, and institutions.

I would like to dream out loud about what could happen as a large number of Southern Baptists respond to the call to be servant leaders.

Team Leadership

Servant leaders are team people. When work is accomplished among Southern Baptists by those who have a deep concern for people and a sense of urgency for productive achievement, then there is a common feeling that unites individual Baptists, their leadership, and the denomination. The goals of the denomination *are* the goals of its people. Mutual trust, respect, and participation raise the level of achievement and fulfillment. When leaders build teamwork, the denomination does not lord it over the people nor do Baptist people neglect and fail to support the churches' work through the denomination. As a team, our leaders will build one another up in order to do a larger, better work for our Lord.

Transforming Leadership

Transforming leadership: (1) recognizes and utilizes existing needs and demands of potential followers, (2) looks for potential motives in followers, (3) seeks to satisfy higher needs, and (4) engages the full energies of the follower. The result of transforming leadership among Baptists would be a relationship of mutual stimulation that converts Baptist followers into leaders and transforms Baptist leaders into spiritual agents of the kingdom of God. Their purposes become fused. Power bases are linked. Such leadership ultimately becomes moral and spiritual in that it raises the level of human conduct and ethical aspiration of both the leader and the led. During this time of transition Southern Baptists need such an experience of transformation.[9]

Moral and Ethical Leadership

Moral leadership has the capacity to rise above the claims of everyday wants, needs, and expectations. Moral and ethical leadership relates leadership behavior—its roles, choices, style, and commitments—to a set of seasoned, conscious values. Even conflict can be a source of value and vital change when mobilized and shaped by gifted leaders. This will be discussed in more detail in chapter 8. Moral leadership reaches into the needs and value structures, mobilizing and directing support for such values as justice, liberty, equality, individual dignity, brotherhood, and world evangelization.

Such moral leadership: (1) operates at need and value levels higher than those of the potential followers but not so much higher as to lose contact, (2) can exploit conflict and tension within persons' value structures, and (3) realigns values and reorganizes institutions where necessary at a higher value level. This leads to authentic denomination renewal.[10]

Visionary Leadership

Renewed and renewing leadership is always working on the future, the big picture, the dreams, the hopes, the aspirations, and the larger purposes of the organization. The visionary lifts up the dream among Southern Baptists and helps them to see a better way. The visionary lifts people's spirits by pointing to a sense of purpose and destiny.

Anyone can find problems. Anyone can work to patch up the mistakes of yesterday. Some can maintain the status quo. But what of tomorrow? Thomas Horton, chief executive officer of the American Management Association, wrote: "The ability to inspire commitment from others in the organization is a fundamental mark of leadership."

Rather than discouraging creativity and change, Southern Baptists have traditionally followed their visionary leaders. We can do no less during these opportune days of Bold Mission Thrust.

True visionary leadership, however, is not ego centered. It's not showy. It is encouraged and disciplined by the command, "Seek first His kingdom and His righteousness" (Matt. 6:33).

Trust Building

Renewed leadership will take on the responsibility of trust building, not simply for the individual leader but within the denomination. Trust is essential to the functioning of a healthy denomination. Cycles of mistrust can be broken and cycles of trust can be established by the intentional action of Baptist leadership. This kind of trust is not blind. Rather, it is trust willingly given because the best interest of the led is being served by the leader. It has been demonstrated that a leader's ability to exercise influence over others is founded on mutual trust. Such trust is promoted by integrity, equity, ability, intention, and reliability.

People Orientation

Southern Baptists will continue to need leaders who care about people, who treat them as made in the image of God with soul freedom and responsibility. Servant leaders put people first—before personal ambition or institutional success. Servant leaders will stay close to and listen to people—really listen to what they say, feel, and want to do for God.

Leaders who really love people are those who will build them up and call forth the best they have. Such leaders will help people realize their dreams.

Encouraging counsel to the Southern Baptist family:

I would encourage Southern Baptists to unite on the basis of making the greatest effort in history to evangelize and minister to a world on the brink of disaster.
Gary Cook, Dir., Church Staff and Support Division, BSSB

Apply the gospel, meet human needs, and publish, teach, write, and speak to that end. Focus attention on lay leaders—both men and women—who have been moved, motivated, and sustained by their Baptist fellowship.
James M. Dunn, Exec. Dir., Baptist Joint Committee on Public Affairs

We must discover anew the servant mentality that is demanded in the Scripture and we must honor those who display such a servant disposition.
Jack B. Johnson, Exec. Dir.-Treas., Arizona

It is a great day for a servant church—a servant Christian! Let us ask God to help us make Jesus Christ Lord of all we have and are and will become! Then, from this servant posture, let us move in God's love and power to wash feet in his name.
Kenneth R. Lyle, Exec. Dir., Maryland

Pay attention to the concerns of vocal extremists but not to the point of taking our eyes off the masses of Southern Baptists who are labeled "moderates" simply because their concerns are down the middle of the road in missions, evangelism, and church growth.
Ernest E. Mosley, Exec. Dir., Illinois

Let Southern Baptist churches and staff members involve themselves in a sharing of their call to ministry. The fragmentation in churches weakens our witnessing ministry to the point of ineptness. Let us rejoice more!
Joe Stacker, Secretary, Church Administration Department, BSSB

The future belongs to the people of God, people who travel the high road where Jesus Christ is Lord, . . . where doing the will of God in daily life is the supreme good.
Foy Valentine, Exec. Dir.-Treas., Christian Life Commmission

We will not build a strong, vibrant force of fourteen million Southern Baptists as a standing spiritual army for God if we tell them in an autocratic way what they must be, do, believe, and support. It is the responsibility of Southern Baptist leaders in every role to lift up our people to a place that is already theirs.

Problem Solving

Leaders are responsible for solving problems if for no other reason than they themselves help create problems. An effective leader will not neglect or avoid problems. Servant leaders are aware that problems exist, but they see in problems opportunities for creative gain and advancement. Leaders may respond to problems emotionally, intuitively, subjectively, or rationally.

The rational approach, which often proves to be most helpful, consists of the following steps: (1) define the problem; (2) define the desired outcome; (3) gather all available information pertinent to the problem; (4) analyze the information; (5) formulate the alternative courses of action; (6) choose the alternative that is most promising; (7) act upon the decision; and (8) monitor, evaluate, and refine the solution. Our Southern Baptist people depend on their leaders to solve problems in such a prayerful and responsible way.

Decision Making

One of the major tasks of leaders is to make decisions. Good leaders are characterized by a high percentage of good decisions. It is crucial in Southern Baptist life that leaders make decisions that are in the long-term best interest of our Baptist family, as well as the whole people of God. We depend on our leaders to make major decisions based on (1) biblical perspectives, (2) the best available data, (3) awareness of future trends, (4) historical perspectives, (5) wise consultation, (6) the best available alternatives, (7) the availability of resources, (8) potential for effective outcome, (9) consequences to the denominational family, and (10) the purpose of the Baptist entities.

Competence

Each place of service and leadership among Southern Baptists requires gifts, talents, and skills given by the Spirit and sharpened by experience. Some places require unusual knowledge, skills, attitudes, background, and competencies.

When I need a medical doctor, I am delighted to find one who is a Christian and a Baptist—but also competent. Baptist leaders are always to be leading, learning, growing, and developing into the best servants we can be for God.

Southern Baptists will continue to have competent leadership as we practice spiritual discernment, common sense, and good business judgment. We have a watchword for competency: "Be diligent to present yourself approved to God as a workman who does not need to be ashamed, handling accurately the word of truth" (2 Tim. 2:15).

Personal Integrity

Integrity is at the top of the list of almost any assessment of leadership. Just what does the leader believe, value, and stand for?

Peter Drucker has written, "Without character, all else is spoiled." The American Management Association, the *Wall Street Journal,* the Gallup Poll, and other sources sound this watchword among leaders: "Integrity!"

The character of a leader is that inner quality of life that is governed by principle rather than mere feeling or outward pressure. Honest, open, straightforward, consistent dealings with others are expressed in the truth, "My word is my bond." Moral and ethical behavior and attitudes that stand the gaze of a gracious but demanding Lord undergird leadership integrity. The Lord said,

"Watch over your heart with all diligence,/For from it flow the springs of life" (Prov. 4:23).

I am convinced that a careful examination of personal integrity on the part of each leader would mature Southern Baptists and silence much of the divisive criticism in our family.

Christian Authenticity

Faith in Jesus Christ as Lord and Savior, a sense of calling in life to serve him, and a complete confidence in the Holy Scripture as the rule of faith and practice are the marks of authenticity among Southern Baptist leaders. One of the greatest blessings of my life has been to work alongside Baptist leaders—well-known and un-known—who gave abundant evidence of God's gracious work in their lives. The life-changing power of Christ in salvation releases us and empowers us to be his servant leaders in the world.

The exciting hope and my expectation for our great denomination is for servant leadership, renewed by the Spirit of God, to be leaven, seed, and bountiful harvest. How we need leaders who are absolutely committed to the renewing of this denomination in its productive service in God's kingdom!

Notes

1. Robert K. Greenleaf, *Servant Leadership* (New York: Paulist Press, 1977), p. 88.

2. Dalton E. McFarland, *Management: Foundations and Practices* (New York: Macmillan Publishing Co., Inc., 1979), pp. 214-215.

3. Paul Hersey and Kenneth H. Blanchard, *Management of Organizational Behavior* (Englewood Cliffs: Prentice-Hall, Inc., 1982), p. 83.

4. James J. Cribbin, *Leadership* (New York: AMACOM, 1981), pp. 12-13.

5. James McGregor Burns, *Leadership* (New York: Harper & Row Publishers, Inc., 1978), p. 18.

6. James L. Sullivan has clearly expressed the distinction between a delegate and a messenger: "Delegates are called by that name because as such they have been given delegated authority and instructions when they leave for an annual meeting. They go to an annual meeting. They vote the way they are told to vote by the churches and technically

can take no other stand. Baptists do not function this way. They send messengers from their churches who come together as Christian fellow-believers, committed but unin-structed, seeking to find and do God's will according to their best judgment as each matter of concern is presented to them and after adequate discussion has been heard from the floor." From *Baptist Polity As I See It* (Nashville: Broadman Press, 1983), p. 45.

7. Robert R. Blake and Jane Srygley Mouton, *The New Managerial Grid* (Houston: Gulf Publishing Company, 1978), p. 11.

8. Greenleaf, p. 10.

9. See Burns, p. 20 for a discussion of this concept.

10. Ibid., pp. 29-46.

6
Communication Strategies

Challenge #6: As a people of God, let us openly communicate with one another in such a way that we share information and knowledge, promote understanding and trust, and advance the work of Christ to which we are mutually committed.

James 3:6-11: The tongue is a fire, the very world of iniquity; the tongue is set among our members as that which defiles the entire body, and sets on fire the course of our life, and is set on fire by hell. For every species of beasts and birds, of reptiles and creatures of the sea, is tamed, and has been tamed by the human race. But no one can tame the tongue; it is a restless evil and full of deadly poison. With it we bless our Lord and Father; and with it we curse men, who have been made in the likeness of God; from the same mouth come both blessing and cursing. My brethren, these things ought not to be this way.
James 1:19: But let everyone be quick to hear, slow to speak and slow to anger.

Organizational Communication: Virtually everyone finds himself temporarily or permanently involved in organizations—schools, churches, hospitals, government agencies, business and military organizations—the list is almost endless.

But just what is an organization?

First, it consists of a *number* of people. . . . Second, it involves *interdependence*. . . . Interdependence calls for *coordination*. . . . And, coordination requires communication. Genesis describes how the building of the Tower of Babel was disrupted by the "confounding of tongues." When men no longer had a common language, when they were unable to communicate, they could not work together.

WILLIAM V. HANEY[1]

129

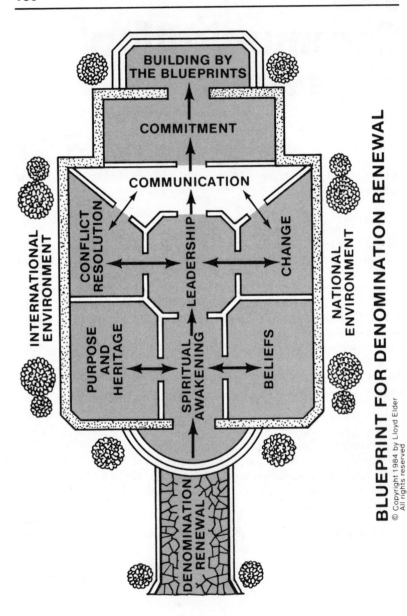

BLUEPRINT FOR DENOMINATION RENEWAL

Renewal of the denomination as an organization requires an effective, comprehensive communication network within the Southern Baptist family.

We must be bold and realistic enough to acknowledge that denomination renewal cannot take place without improved communication. In turn, improved communication cannot result without serious effort on the part of large numbers of Southern Baptists, ministers and laity alike. As in many situations, acknowledgment that a communication problem exists is an essential first step toward solving the problem. Growing up in a large family of fifteen children taught me that some of the communication problems multiply in proportion to the number of persons living together in a family. In a much larger sense, how does the communication problem show itself within the denominational family?

- Through increased tension in the denomination;
- Through unintentional misunderstandings, large and small;
- Through distrust of leadership;
- Through formation of single-issue groups;
- Through failure to maintain consensus on basic Baptist beliefs;
- Through non-Christian response to solving our real problems.

Certainly not all of our denominational ailments can be ascribed to poor communication. It is, however, a major contributor in many respects.

In this chapter, let us examine the communication process, our denominational systems of communication, and the kind of communication channels that will be necessary for renewal.

Communication Process

Carl I. Hovland has defined communication as "the process by which an individual (the communicator) transmits stimuli (usually verbal stimuli) to modify the behavior of other individuals (communicatees)."[2]

Although this definition may be excessively bookish and perhaps too simple, it contains elements that need to be stressed: communication is a *process* which requires *results* (change of mind showing itself in change of behavior) in order to be successful.

Particularly important is the *intended result* of communication. Unless the behavior of the receiver is modified, communication has not taken place. Herein lies the problem of many public speakers, preachers among us included. We confuse *presentation* of the message with *communication* of that message. We equate the fact that we have spoken to an audience with the belief that the message has really penetrated the consciousness of the audience. However, unless behavior has changed, we have failed in our effort to communicate.

For example, the trite comment, "I enjoyed your message" is probably not at all the response the preacher has sought. He exhorted, appealed, interpreted Scripture, and sought to move his congregation to the very depths of their beings. He worked and prayed and perspired to deliver a meaningful sermon—only to hear, "I enjoyed your message."

Lest we be guilty of violating our own principle, however, let us note that it is possible that the person who makes such a response may not be at fault at all! Perhaps this individual just doesn't know how to express feelings accurately. Perhaps he or she is simply responding at a basic level, maybe using words that he or she has heard someone else say on similar occasions. Perhaps the relationship with the preacher is not open enough or deep enough for a more substantial response to be made. Communication becomes even more complex outside the local church and in the context of the denomination.

Beyond the need to understand communication in terms of its intended impact on the receiver is the necessity to perceive it as a *process*. Communication does not exist in isolation. It is not a single point in time. It is a skill, even an art form, that must be nurtured and developed. If the citizens of this nation were to engage in an emphasis on communication as thoroughly as we are enmeshed in the physical fitness craze, we would be enriched indeed! The same thing may be true in our great denomination!

It might be well at this point to examine briefly a communications model. The simplest model involves a sender, a message, and a receiver. I have adapted a model developed by a communications consultant, Don Hill (see Figure 6-1). It deals with:

1. A *message* which is
2. understood by its *sender,* and is
3. *transmitted* through
4. a *medium,* to
5. a *receiver* who understands the message and acts on the basis of this understanding.

The model emphasizes a fact that is overlooked or obscured by many models: the message must be first *understood* by the sender. A preacher cannot communicate God's word without first understanding it. A lawyer cannot communicate his argument unless he understands his client's position. A television newscaster cannot communicate the news unless he or she understands it. If he or she doesn't, the emphasis may be wrong and the information may be miscommunicated. The same is true of any number of communicators within our denomination.

If we are to use effectively the communication process, we need to have a comprehension of all the elements involved. If the sender's understanding of the message is a key component, the sender's understanding of the receiver is also critical to success.

One-to-one, face-to-face communication is most effective because the sender can know the receiver, get instant feedback, and then adjust his message if necessary to produce the desired results. As the number in the audience increases, so does the difficulty of communication. As the medium of communication moves from face-to-face to more impersonal channels, difficulties increase. As the opportunity for immediate, direct feedback from the receiver to the sender decreases, so does the chance of successful communication.

Figure 6-1. Congruent Communication

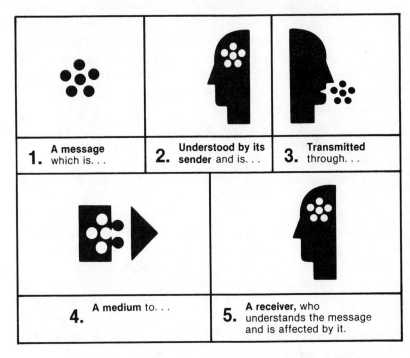

1. A message which is. . .

2. Understood by its sender and is. . .

3. Transmitted through. . .

4. A medium to. . .

5. A receiver, who understands the message and is affected by it.

Communication Factors Among Southern Baptists

How are these factors demonstrated in our denomination?

1. There are a lot of senders: more than 36,000 pastors; other church staff members; SBC, state, and associational leaders; consultants; and representatives.

2. There are millions of messages that need to be transmitted: evangelistic messages, stewardship messages, missions, education, counseling, denominational emphases, menus for the

Wednesday night supper, budget information, calendar dates, schedule times, inspiration, and condolences.

3. There are large numbers of media through which these messages may be sent: word of mouth, preaching, state papers, church newsletters, radio, television, daily newspapers, neighborhood newspapers, visits, denominational publications and telephone.

4. There are many filters which stand between the sender of the message and the receiver: language problems, cultural filters, emotions, prejudices, traditions, illiteracy, apathy, and Christian maturity—or the lack of it.

5. Sending a message toward a receiver is not the same as getting the message through to the receiver. Important announcements are placed in the church newsletter, on bulletin boards, in the state Baptist paper, and are shared in other ways. Still there are those who never get the word.

These are not all the factors that complicate communication. The list simply illustrates the dimensions of our denominational communication problem. And it becomes more and more obvious what difficulty we have at working together as a Southern Baptist organization if our communication system is not working for us.

If you really want to probe more fully the complex scope of denominational communication, study Figure 6-2.

Lippitt in his work on organization renewal defines interfacing as "a combination of dialogue, confrontation, search, and coping." He sees it as a "a process involving internalizing of communication so that something other than information is transmitted."[3] Really, he is asking, as Hovland did in the definition we used earlier in this chapter, for modification of behavior as a criterion for whether communication has taken place.

Even this brief exploration of the communication process shows its practical application to denominational life. A larger number of Southern Baptists needs to be aware of these complex-

FIGURE 6-2. Various Levels of Interfacing

The diagram suggests the many levels at which interfacing takes place. It is a process that involves man at all levels of his existence. Note that

1. **A** and **B** are both sender and receiver in the process of interfacing.
2. Interfacing participants are constantly **processing** through their senses, feelings, ideas, and actions.
3. Interfacing is essentially a dynamic **transaction** with active participation by **A** and **B.**
4. **A** and **B** may be any combination of Individual, Group, Organization, Community, or Nation.
5. **Ecology** describes the complex totality of forces acting on biological man.

SOURCE: Gordon L. Lippitt, ORGANIZATION RENEWAL: Achieving Viability in a Changing World, © 1969, p. 127. Reprinted by permission of Prentice-Hall, Englewood Cliffs, New Jersey.

ities in order to see that the solutions to our problems are possible but not simple. All of us cannot engage in the intensive study that would be necessary to make us communication experts. We can, however, know of some of the important principles and key elements of effective communication. We can be alert to pitfalls. And we can set some goals toward which we may work.

Southern Baptist Communication Channels

How about the channels of communication available to Southern Baptists? They are many. They are diverse. They are highly developed.

1. Some of the most significant channels are the annual meeting of the SBC and the annual meetings of the thirty-seven state conventions. Here are platforms from which utterances are relayed across our land and throughout the world with significant impact on Baptist behavior. Here are arenas where pastors from churches large and small may discuss current denominational issues in private and in public. Here we find opportunities for denominational statesmanship, as well as denominational politics.

Our patterns of communication must be true to the gospel we believe and share. In extreme cases, we do sometimes forget that. How much true communication can take place when speakers are shouted down, when signals are given for voting, when applause and boos echo in the arenas of these meetings during discussion and debate, when facts are loosely dealt with and patience seems to be the rarest of commodities? Most Southern Baptists expect responsible, productive communication from those of us who would claim their attention.

Denomination renewal will not come until we stop shouting *across* each other and begin to have responsible dialogue and interchange *with* each other. We need to recover what Reuel Howe, in the book published several years ago, called "The Miracle of Dialogue."

2. Another major denominational channel is the network of thirty-seven state Baptist papers. News, inspirational material, Bible study, and letters to the editor give interested readers an opportunity to stay current with the vital issues and developments of the day. Technical advances and skilled personnel have shortened the time between event and publication. They are faithful to the task of communicating issues that should engage the attention of the denomination.

3. Now we have inaugurated the most sophisticated and far-reaching technological channel of all—the satellite transmission of television programs to homes from ACTS (American Christian Television System) and to churches, associations, state conventions, and denominational agencies through BTN (Baptist Telecommunication Network).

We have learned how to make available the channels of communication. We have financed them and harnessed them. Yet we still have work to do in assuring that the messages we send are really understood and appropriately acted upon. As the late Edward R. Murrow, a talented communicator, once said,

> We shall expand our communications; we shall orbit our satellites; we shall transmit our message to the world. But, in the end, we shall still deal with the basic elements of human communications; words and pictures. Space satellites and wider world communications will not make it any better. They will simply diffuse it over a wider area—and more quickly.[4]

4. Southern Baptists have achieved a remarkable degree of sophistication in using the mass media of communication available to us today. We have learned to use these media, and we have been aggressive in developing new lines of communication as they have become available. Yet there seems to be a missing ingredient. As Morrow suggested, we are communicating faster and over a wider area but not necessarily better.

5. We have learned to work with and through the daily press in a professional way to communicate our plans and express our opinions. Is there a vote to liberalize liquor laws? Baptist opinion is sought and published. Is there a move to legalize gambling or horse racing and dog racing? Baptists are invited to serve on fact-finding commissions and have a voice in the outcome. The Southern Baptist voice is heard in the halls of Congress and in state legislatures throughout this great country.

6. We have mastered the technicalities of the print and electronic media. Almost every church has equipment with which to

address its members and prospects through a printed newsletter mailed regularly. We excel at arranging conferences, seminars, retreats, and rallies where techniques of communicating the gospel are shared and where we learn to become better church leaders and members.

7. We communicate formally and informally. How much Baptist business is done by telephone? More than we can count. What is the fastest means of Southern Baptist communication? The grapevine—the rumor mill—the corridor gossip. Our denomination has almost limitless resources for sending messages, yet the message is often never received or understood. Why? Let us examine several barriers which seem to block understanding.

Built-In Barriers to Communication

Perhaps the most significant barrier is our *polity.* This we would never change. But we must understand its communication characteristics in order that we might change it from a stumbling block to a stepping-stone.

Let us consider for a moment our denomination as if it were a single organization—hierarchical in polity. (Please note carefully that this is an illustration, not a recommendation!) The president would communicate with the state executive secretaries and the agency heads. The state executives would pass the word to their staff and to the associational directors of missions. Agency heads would get the word to their employees. Associational directors of missions would get the message to the pastors, who, in turn, would communicate it to their staff and congregation. Efficient, effective, fast. The message would be monitored every step of the way to make sure it was being sent faithfully. The response would be carefully audited to make sure the faithful were receiving it as it was intended. We could even devise a system of penalties for failure to respond in an appropriate manner.

We recognize, of course, that Southern Baptist communication is not at all like that—nor would we ever permit it to be. The Convention president may make a far-reaching, consequence-laden suggestion. But since we are fond of saying that no Baptist can speak for another, that is just what it is—a suggestion. Many may favor it, and many others find fault with it. The pastor may or may not feel the suggestion ought to be given favorable response in the congregation. And even if he should respond favorably, the congregation may be contrary-minded! Our polity is a major barrier to effective communications in the sense described.

Unwarranted assumptions also block communication. Because a leader uses certain words or is a member of certain organizations, assumptions may be made which do not square with the facts. When this happens, his communication—and thus his performance—suffers. A pastor is perceived to spend too much (or too little) time in his study or in visitation or in community affairs. Unwarranted assumptions people hold concerning their pastor may cripple his communication and his ministry.

Failure to listen—to really listen—is another major barrier to communication. This is especially significant in a group whose professionals are trained to talk but not to listen, except perhaps in counseling situations. Or we do selective listening. We hear what we want to hear, which is not necessarily what the sender of the message says or writes or means by gesture.

I was raised in a large family. When we have a family reunion, we have to rent a family life center. Also, we like to talk a lot. (I'm the quietest one in the family—being one of the youngest.) Jokingly we have said that we have to hire outsiders to come to the family reunion to do the listening!

How similar this is to our denomination. Are we at a point where hired, trained, objective listeners would enhance our experience of renewal? In order to be straightforward in our attempts at denominational understanding, let me highlight some additional barriers that make our communication difficult.

Quantity of message. We know that the quality of messages is important, but the astronomical quantity of messages to which we are exposed as a denomination compounds the problem. The Sunday School Board itself generates an astounding number of

Encouraging counsel to the Southern Baptist family:

Let's focus our efforts on the mission of Christ on earth—to preach and teach the gospel of Christ to the world. Further, let us train and develop the disciples of Christ in the way of righteousness. Southern Baptists should lift up the body of Christ with its interdependence, submitting to the headship of Christ.
John H. Allen, Exec. Dir.-Treas., Alaska

These years we have left in the twentieth century can be magnificent years of accomplishment for Southern Baptists. We must let nothing interfere with the priority we have given to Bold Mission Thrust. The momentum which has been building must be accelerated. Using the benefits of satellite communications, we must give our best efforts to sharing the good news with the whole world. God will bless our efforts. If we are faithful, history may well reveal that these were Southern Baptists' finest years.
Jimmy D. Edwards, V.-Pres. for Publishing and Distribution, BSSB

The great years of the Southern Baptist Convention are not behind us but are before us. Let's do a better job of *telling our story* of what we are doing for missions, educational, and benevolent causes of our Convention.
James N. Griffith, Jr., Exec. Sec.-Treas., Georgia

Remember there is strength in diversity. The genius of Southern Baptists has been cooperation in a common goal—winning the world to Jesus Christ—in spite of differences.
Lloyd T. Householder, Dir., Office of Communications, BSSB

We must close the gap which has developed between our agencies and Southern Baptist people. It may be a credibility gap or a feeling of distance. The fact is that we are all one, and we must be careful to experience that oneness.
H. Franklin Paschall, President, SBC, 1967-1969

messages. Other agencies, state conventions, associations, and churches churn out oral and written messages at a flow rivaling Niagara Falls. Selecting those from among the flood that ought to be heeded becomes a staggering task for the receiver.

Complexity. We have a nonsystem of communication in Baptist life that is complex and confusing. Whom do we trust? To whom do we choose to listen? Are signals from different sources contradictory? The confounded, confused receiver may give up and simply stop trying to untangle the complex web of communication.

Inference and assumptions. We do not often examine our inferences and assumptions as carefully as the passenger on a train once did. "That's certainly a good-looking herd of brown cows, isn't it?" his seatmate observed. "Well, they're brown on one side, anyhow," he replied. He didn't want to make unwarranted assumptions. We need to check our inferences and assumptions carefully to make certain they are correct.

Closed minds. "Don't confuse me with the facts. My mind is made up." This is too often the attitude of many Southern Baptists. We seem to panic at the possibility of revising a long-held concept or changing our minds because of new information. Renewal is blocked when the mind remains closed.

Cultural diversity. Southern Baptists used to be simply Southern and Baptist. Today we are black, white, yellow, red, and tan. We are Northern, Eastern, Western, Southern. We are Hispanic, Oriental, American Indian, European, and Daughters of the American Revolution. Cultural diversity has exploded whatever cultural unity we used to have. Such diversity means we have to work harder to develop mutual understanding, trust, and Christian fellowship.

Developing Strategic Communications

Given the complexity of the communication process, the special problems caused by our polity, and the multitude of barriers that block effective communication, what steps can we take to work toward denomination renewal through better communication strategies?

As with every other aspect of renewal, this must begin with individual commitment. You and I must first recognize that there is a problem. We must then give ourselves wholeheartedly to becoming part of the solution rather than being a part of the problem.

Following one of his parables, Jesus indirectly commended the worldly wise as being more shrewd than the sons of light. In the matter of communication, it could well be that people who have a purely secular orientation are in many cases better communicators than we Christians are. They don't deny that their primary motivation is self-interest. Even with self-interest as their dominant motive, these people recognize that open, skillful communication is the best policy.

In their stimulating study of North American corporations, Thomas J. Peters and Robert H. Waterman, Jr., observed eight attributes found in those companies they considered excellent. As they presented their analysis to one corporate executive, he responded by saying, "There's only one thing wrong with your excellent company analysis. You need a ninth principle—communications. We just plain talk to each other a lot without a lot of paper or formal rigmarole."[5]

When Peters and Waterman wrote their book, they observed that in excellent companies there is a lot of open communication and that it is a factor which is highly motivating to employees. Where there is a lot of open communication, people are motivated to buy into what's being done. Imagine the impact on Bold Mission Thrust of this kind of communication among Southern Baptists!

If those who are wise in the ways of the world recognize the necessity of good communications, how much more should we Christians. *Communication* literally means *together one*. We Christians confess one Lord. In him we have a basis for communication that those apart from Christ don't have.

As we grow in the grace of Christ, we come closer and closer to realizing God's desire that we love our neighbors as ourselves. As we grow in our love, we grow in our desire to hear and understand what they are thinking and feeling—what is important to them.

As we grow in the grace of Christ, we know more and more what Paul understood when he compared the church to a human body. Paul said it was a good thing that the parts of the body were different from each other. He asked the Corinthians to imagine what it would be like if the body were just one big eye. If it were just an eye, the body couldn't feel, hear, or move around.

Diversity in the parts of the human body is part of what makes it a wonderful creation. And yet all of these diverse parts are linked together and centrally controlled by the head.

So it should be in the church. We are diverse. But that's the way God intended it. There's tremendous strength and creativity in diversity when all of the different parts are linked to each other through Christ. Let Paul's vision be ours. Let us not only give assent to it but let us live it out. Here are some practical things we can do to realize God's will for his people in this matter of communication:

- Make a commitment to integrity in communication, personally and within the denomination.
- Make a personal commitment to listen to what others mean, not just to what they say or write.
- Consciously, deliberately become a student of the communication process.
- Use faithfully and regularly the communication channels available, both denominational and those outside the denomination.
- Consider the barriers to communication and help to tear them down one by one.
- Believe that communication can help change the climate of the Southern Baptist denomination.

- Approach communication in a spirit of reconciliation rather than in a spirit of harsh condemnation.
- In motivational communication, recognize the receiver's freedom in Christ and so avoid manipulative tactics.
- Seek the personal spiritual growth that diminishes prejudice, builds trust, avoids being judgmental, and seeks the common good.
- Act on our spiritual unity in Christ. Let our communications proceed from a heart bathed in much prayer. Let us see those with whom we communicate as being important parts of Christ's body, the church.

A communications strategy within our denomination, as within any organization, depends upon at least two kinds of channels: (1) the formal system and (2) the informal system. In it all we shall be held accountable for every idle word. In the effort to experience denomination renewal, both these systems need to be renewed and controlled by the deepest desire to communicate effectively the eternal gospel of Jesus Christ in a chaotic world!

Notes

1. William V. Haney, *Communication and Organizational Behavior* (Homewood, Illinois: Richard D. Irwin, Inc., 1967), pp. 9-10.

2. Carl I. Hovland, Irving L. Janis, and Harold H. Kelley, *Communication and Persuasion* (New Haven: Yale University Press, 1953), p. 12.

3. Gordon L. Lippitt, *Organization Renewal* (New York: Meredith Corporation, 1969), p. 125.

4. Quoted in *Public Relations News,* Oct. 2, 1961.

5. Thomas J. Peters and Robert H. Waterman, Jr., *In Search of Excellence* (New York: Harper & Row, Publishers, Inc., 1982), p. 123.

7
Shaping
Change

Challenge #7: As a people of God, let us understand change as normal and inevitable in all human experience and let us seek to shape change as our denomination participates with God in his great creative and redemptive work.

Genesis 1:27-28: And God created man in His own image, in the image of God He created him; male and female He created them. And God blessed them; and God said to them, "Be fruitful and multiply, and fill the earth, and subdue it; and rule over the fish of the sea and over the birds of the sky, and over every living thing that moves on the earth."
Hebrews 13:8: Jesus Christ is the same yesterday and today, yes and forever.

Planning for Change: Organization development is designed to improve the health of an organization and to increase the capability of the organization to achieve its goals. This means goals rather than roles, collaboration rather than competition, and ideas rather than personalities are emphasized in decision-making process. In brief, it is an effort to help an organization develop its own capacity for self-renewal. . . . Organization development is a response to change, it includes a strategy for planned change and the primary focus is on the human side of the enterprise.

LYLE E. SCHALLER[1]

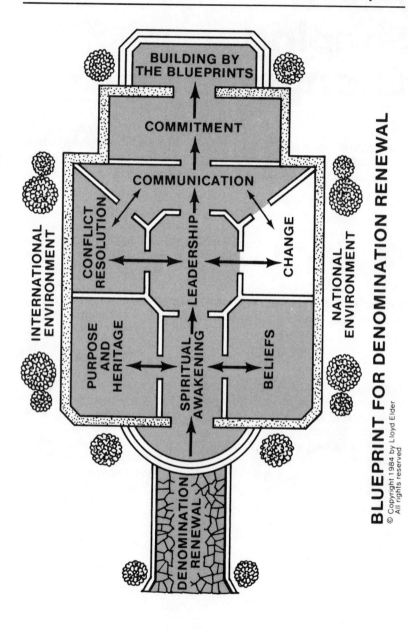

BLUEPRINT FOR DENOMINATION RENEWAL

Denomination renewal depends on our shaping change. The ways in which individuals and groups handle change are vital indications of their maturity, stability, and openness to growth. Those who are dominated by fear or even dread of change are in trouble. So are those who are obsessed with change for its own sake. The key to dealing with change is to shape it, much as our denomination sought to do in the "Shaping the 70s" and "Impact 80s" efforts. Another key is to differentiate between change that is good and change that is not. Change could be added to death and taxes on my list of the inevitable.

Change is sometimes pleasant, sometimes unpleasant. Some change comes in situations of rejoicing, others in crisis situations. We undergo personal changes physically, emotionally, and spiritually. Some of us do not change in the proper way at the proper time. We experience changes in family life. Some of our change results from illness.

These personal kinds of change, as important as they are, are not the kinds of change we shall be considering in this chapter. Rather, we are looking at a healthy, positive, corporate change leading to denomination renewal. This blueprint challenges us to deal with denominational change: its facts, face, fear, function, and force.

The Fact of Change

Perhaps we need not dwell too long on the fact of change. Surely we realize that without change we would be:

- walking rather than soaring into space and back via space shuttle;
- warming our caves with kindling rather than conditioning our homes with heat pumps;
- scribbling in the sand rather than punching our manuscripts into word processors;
- stalking and stabbing our food rather than purchasing it at the supermarket;

- squinting at the sun to tell time rather than glancing at a digital wristwatch.
- riding to conventions primarily by trains rather than by air.

The importance of the last-named illustration of change was underscored not too long after the industrial revolution. Various business enterprises learned to their distress, and in some cases with accompanying economic disaster, the consequences of failing to deal with the fact of change.

The railroads, for example, eighty years ago held a monopoly on moving goods and people. They thought it would be good enough to remain in the railroad business. They failed to face the fact of change and to see that they should have been in the transportation business rather than just the railroad business. They expanded their lines and built more engines and laid more track. But the airlines and trucking industries took over the market because they understood the reality of change in the transportation business.

Earlier the buggy manufacturers failed to survive the horse-and-buggy days and the automobile took over. They saw themselves as buggy makers, not as people movers, and change buried them.

Our denomination, too, must learn these lessons and decide what "business" we are in. We know that we must be about the Lord's business. But is our main business that of defining doctrine, being loyal to our denomination, controlling a Convention, or defending academic freedom? Or, is our main business to follow the lordship of Christ, build trust and maturity among the people of God, agree upon evangelistic and missionary efforts, and seek to encourage a mighty host of Southern Baptist people to work at this business?

We have felt the impact of undesired and undesirable change. Now, we need to deal with the fact of that change and reexamine our eternal purposes with a view to restoring some of the vitality with which our Baptist forebears pursued the basic tasks of our denomination. Can we agree that we are still responsible to God and to one another for *"eliciting, combining, and directing the energies of the Baptist denomination of Christians for the propagation of the Gospel, any law, usage, or custom to the contrary notwithstanding"?*

For nearly 140 years this statement of purpose from the charter of the Southern Baptist Convention has stood unchanged. Even more so, the gospel we proclaim is changeless. The world about us has changed. Our methods and materials have changed. We have changed in many ways as people—but our purpose should be changeless, and our energies should be unswervingly dedicated to its accomplishment.

The Face of Change

John Naisbitt, in his book *Megatrends,* has captured in a few words a portrait of the face of change in America over the past half-century. Naisbitt sees a restructuring of America that is having an impact on both our inner and outer lives. Major changes can be seen in the following ten areas, according to Naisbitt:

"1. Although we continue to think we live in an industrial society, we have, in fact, changed to an economy based on the creation and distribution of information.

2. We are moving in the dual directions of high tech/high touch, matching each new technology with a compensatory human response.

3. No longer do we have the luxury of operating in an isolated, self-sufficient national economic system; we must now acknowledge that we are part of a global economy. We have begun to let go of the idea that the United States is and must remain the world's industrial leader as we move on to other tasks.

4. We are restructuring from a society run by short-term considerations and rewards in favor of dealing with things in much longer time frames.

5. In cities and states and small organizations and subdivisions, we have rediscovered the ability to act innovatively and to achieve results—from the bottom up.

6. We are shifting from institutional help to more self-reliance in all aspects of our lives.

7. We are discovering that the framework of representative democracy has become obsolete in an era of instantaneously shared information.

8. We are giving up our dependence on the hierarchical structures in favor of informal networks. This will be especially important in the business community.

9. More Americans are living in the South and West, leaving behind the old industrial cities of the North.

10. From a narrow either/or society with a limited range of personal choices, we are exploding into a freewheeling, multi-option society."[2]

Naisbitt concludes that we are living in a time of parenthesis—a time between eras, between past and future, neither here nor there; that America is restructuring, not breaking up, but rebuilding from the bottom up into a stronger, more balanced society with new challenges and possibilities.

These trends which Naisbitt has identified make up the setting and environment in which we live as a denomination. Such trends portray in some measure the face of change for Southern Baptists.

Another commentator on change, Daniel Yankelovich, in *New Rules,* compares the changes in our society with the geological formations under the earth's surface, giant plates. Sometimes these plates shift their positions as they grind against each other. Although slight, the shifts cause volcanoes and earthquakes on the surface even years later.

Yankelovich considers that the struggle in our society, the very leading edge of a genuine cultural revolution, is the search for "self-fulfillment in a world turned upside down." This quest often collides violently with traditional rules, creating a large-scale battle of values. Yankelovich says graphically that "millions of Americans are hungry to live their lives to the brim, determined to consume every dish on the smorgasbord of human experience."[3]

This desire for self-fulfillment may not be supported by the economic environment. Yankelovich sees the following obvious flaw in people's strategies for self-fulfillment: "The desires of most Americans to move toward expanded choice, pluralism of life styles and greater freedom, while the economy, besieged by inflation and recession, moves relentlessly in the opposite direction—toward restriction of choice."[4]

Yet another astute observer of change, Philip Lesly, points out the difference between past and present patterns of change (see Figure 7-1). Every element affects every other element.[5]

As a denomination, we need to understand that an undetected shift beneath the surface years ago may be causing tremors in the fellowship today and rumbles for the coming years. Some among us need to be carefully studying these almost imperceptible movements so that there may be sounded the notes of caution, understanding, and even hope in the midst of change.

The face of change in our society is, without question, the environment and, at times, the forerunner of change in our denomination. We would show extreme wisdom and stewardship of the gospel if we would not let every issue of a pluralistic and secular society be fought out inside the fellowship of our denomination and on the platform of our conventions. We would do better to unite persistently in the challenge to call our society to the judgment and grace of the gospel than to become the judge of all society's economic and political ills.

The face of change in our denomination sometimes concerns me:

- from a confession of faith toward creedalism of doctrine;
- from decisions out of fellowship and trust toward decisions by pressure and politics;
- from mission work by the convention method to projects by the society method;
- from the strength of denominational heritage toward the power base of multiple independent approaches;

FIGURE 7-1.

PAST PATTERNS OF CHANGE

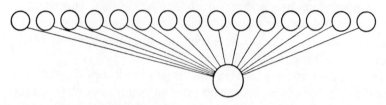

Old patterns of change, in which one key element was likely to be changing materially at one time. Other elements responded to the alteration of the changing one.

PRESENT PATTERNS OF CHANGE

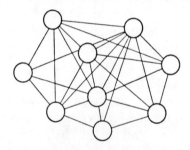

New patterns of change, in which many elements are changing at the same time, and all are influencing each other's changes.

From THE PEOPLE FACTOR by Philip Lesly. Homewood, IL: Dow Jones-Irwin, Copyright © 1974, pp. 36-37. Reproduced by permission of Philip Lesly Company, Consultants on Public Relations and Public Affairs, Chicago, IL.

- from emphasis on the local church to the rise of glamorous television and parachurch enterprises;
- from a ministry of many Baptist brethren toward undue attention to the charismatic leadership of a few; and
- from institutions created by and for the denomination toward institutions with private purposes.

The face of change in our denomination, however, has its positive side:

- a renewed interest in doctrine;
- an upsurge of volunteerism in missions;
- a focus of attention on polity and heritage;
- a call to trusteeship and accountability in the institutions;
- a corrective move toward biblical conservatism; and
- the reaffirmation of the priesthood of all believers.

The Fear of Change

Change—whether good or bad, planned or unplanned, expected or unexpected, trivial or significant—is often perceived by the individual as threatening. Routines are disturbed, habits are reformed, traditions are shattered, complacency is challenged. These disturbances, reformations, and challenges produce fear.

In the face of the most radical change of all, the change from unbeliever to believer in Jesus Christ as Savior and Lord, how many turn away sadly after the manner of the rich, young ruler? Here, as in many other instances, the fear lies in the unwillingness to make the sacrifice demanded of the followers of Christ.

Even though most of us experience change with at least some discomfort, fear need not paralyze us. Acknowledging our humanity can open us up to the power and love of God and remind us to walk by faith, not by sight. As Elaine Dickson has said so well, "Life is change—chosen by us or forced on us. The earth does shift as we walk on it. New conditions are being established regularly in our lives. Something new is being exchanged for something old. Shifts in direction are occurring. . . . Our lives keep changing."[6]

Most of us fear what we do not know. If as individuals we become familiar with change and accept its inevitability, we can deal with it in a mature manner. The same is true of organizational change in churches and in our denomination. If this is true, why should we be frightened of change? Why should we try to hide in our foxholes of self-satisfaction, expecting the winds of change to blow over our heads, leaving us untouched? The answers are deep in the roots of human nature. We resist anything that requires us to revise the comfortable patterns of our lives.

For example, one church which tried change recently was subjected to extreme community pressure. A Baptist congregation in a major metropolitain area tried to take seriously the request from the mayor of the city that the churches help with a large number of homeless persons in the city.

The church proposed opening temporary shelter for six homeless women in the winter season. The pastor received angry protests from some members of the community and elected officials. In light of the turmoil, the church abandoned the project. A statement issued by the pastor cited "obscene and abusive opposition" which "reached the point of intimations of violence." Here is a congregation which tried to take seriously the call of Christ to feed the hungry, provide water for the thirsty, and give hospitality to the stranger. Yet, fear of change dominated the emotions of the people in the community.

Southern Baptists need not fear change. Rather, if John Naisbitt is on target in his book *Megatrends,* we may be moving into our best era.

1. Baptists need not fear the information society. Rather, we have been, are now, and will continue to be in the information business—not just any information but the *truth* that makes persons free. We must improve our effectiveness in internal information exchange. Also, our people must penetrate every arena of the information society.

2. Baptists need not fear forced technology. Rather, let us be good stewards of it in order to share widely the Christian message. The high tech/high touch society must find Baptists providing the high touch needs of the human spirit in the Christian family, the gathered congregation, the caring touch of an undershepherd ministry, and trust-building relationships within the denomination.

Encouraging counsel to the Southern Baptist family:

Remember our Baptist heritage as a foundation for creating our immediate future.
Mancil Ezell, Secretary, Church Media Library Department, BSSB

The recent unrest in the denomination has produced significant reaffirmation of biblical loyalty. If we can rally afresh around our Baptist distinctives and the Cooperative Program emphasis to undergird Bold Missions, then our greatest years of ministry are ahead, not behind.
Darold H. Morgan, President, Annuity Board, SBC

Let us major on the majors. We need more continuity in programming. Also, there needs to be more tolerance on the part of all.
Baptists need to keep in mind that facts and truths are not the same. Facts change and reports of them must change. Truth is eternal and is just as valid now as when Christ walked the earth in human flesh.
James L. Sullivan, President, SBC, 1976-1977

We need a new commitment to communicate the gospel to modern man in the language of today. No change in doctrine but a change in methods is needed. We need for worship to be a celebration but not liturgical. We need expository, biblical preaching from the Word of God. Let us depend on the supernatural work of the Holy Spirit to work miracles in our fellowships.
Jaroy Webber, President, SBC, 1975-1977

Abandon the effort to make clones of everyone. Instead, love ourselves and others as persons created by God in his image and devote ourselves to developing the persons God created under his purposeful direction.
E. DeVaughn Woods, V.-Pres. of Finance, Office of Finance, BSSB

3. As Christians, our people must not fear the trend toward a global society. Rather, let us continue to be *world Christians,* loving the world for which Christ died, working for world peace, and undergirding the far-flung work of our Foreign Mission Board.

4. It is good news, not bad news, that one megatrend is toward long-term considerations. There should be no fear—rather renewed hope—in an enlarged vision, strategic planning, and concerted action. We must not live from personality to personality, issue to issue, nor from Convention to Convention. Rather, as Baptists we must ask ourselves these questions: What business are we in? Where do we want to be in the kingdom work five years from now? How do we get there from here?

5. The trend toward decentralization holds no dread for Baptists. Baptists have a decentralized structure with fourteen million Baptists, thirty-six thousand churches, twelve hundred associations, thirty-seven state conventions, and their institutions, the Southern Baptist Convention, and its twenty agencies and institutions. But there is a two-edged warning here: (1) A centralized creedal structure could become a destructive flaw in Baptist life. (2) Constructive decentralization among Southern Baptists will require a strong central core of shared causes, meanings, beliefs, and values.

6. The denomination must not be afraid of the trend toward self-help and away from institutional help. Rather, our institutions must be servant organizations, fulfilling their denominational purposes, standing for the dignity of persons, advocating fiercely the priesthood of the believer, and facilitating the efforts of persons in moving toward more autonomy and self-help.

7. The trend from representative democracy toward participatory democracy has affected our denomination, just as it has affected society in general. Shall the "Baptist establishment" be frightened by this direction or shall we (1) make it easier for individuals to participate, (2) draw a larger membership into the decision-making processes of the denomination, (3) encourage

lay participation at all levels, (4) provide information openly, honestly, and without being defensive, and (5) practice responsible, knowledgeable participation?

8. John Naisbitt reports a trend away from hierarchies toward "networking" in American society. Of all people, Baptists should not press for a hierarchy but implement the genius of our polity. The large number of components of our denomination have the potential of being amazingly effective as a network. Or, we can also become a flawed, fragmented denomination. The value of Baptist members and churches, acceptance of the diversity of gifts, fulfillment of program assignments, and the encouragement of responsible risks can all be channeled into great goal achievement.

9. Southern Baptists can either fear the migration from North to South or we can thank God for the population growth in our "Baptist stronghold." In our older state conventions, Baptists must gear up for witness, outreach, evangelism, discipling, church planting, and utilization of our Baptist work force. Changes will cause Baptists to adapt methodology and traditional ways, join forces with the newer state conventions, and make effective use of telecommunication technology (ACTS and BTN) to be both person- and growth-oriented.

10. Perhaps the trend that terrifies us the most is the coming era of multiple choices. We have moved from a time when things were simple, when it was a question of either/or, when things were black or white. But again, fear of change is no substitute for faith in God. People need basic structure and stability during times of ambiguity and transition. We need to be held firmly by biblical principles. We must confess our faith, teach our people Christian basics, and trust each other with the freedom of choice in America's multi-option society.

The Function of Change

The true function of change is progress. Change that is regressive is undesirable. Change for the sake of change is wasted energy. Change that is too rapid is "neither natural or good for people or organizations."[7] Too little or too much change is dangerous.

As hard as it is to believe, it has been two decades since Alvin Toffler named a reality we were then and still are having to face: *future shock.*

> The acceleration of change in our time is, itself, an elemental force. The accelerative thrusts has personal and psychological, as well as sociological consequences. . . . The book argues forcefully, I hope, that, unless man quickly learns to control the rate of change in his personal affairs as well as in society at large, we are doomed to a massive adaptional breakdown.[8]

If the function of change is progress, the nature of the organization is a key factor in achieving this progress. In the preceding chapter on communication, I suggested that since our denomination is not hierarchial it is an inefficient vehicle for communication. For the same reason, it is an inefficient vehicle for change. In a clinical sense, we are what Michael A. Berger calls an "organized anarchy." We share this description with other human services organizations. Such organizations are characterized by "ambiguous goals, unclear and contested technologies, strong norms against evaluation, and unstable participation by decision makers."[9]

Although this academic language may not seem entirely appropriate, can we not see a helpful linkage between the volunteer structure of our denomination and Berger's "organized anarchy"? This is an insightful characterization of our unique polity and its contemporary expressions. Yet, there is help for such organizations if the following four steps are followed in seeking change:

    (1) concentrate efforts,

    (2) learn the history,

    (3) build a coalition, and

    (4) use the formal and informal systems.

These tactics are related closely to the suggestion I will make in the following section on "The Force of Change."

Still another contemporary concept used to describe the nature of our denomination is found in organization studies—"network." A network may be understood as the purposeful, productive interdependence and interrelationship of otherwise autonomous organizations working on broad goals and objectives. Change may function to strengthen ties and multiply production within the network. James L. Sullivan described the same phenomenon when he said that we as a denomination are "a rope of sand with the strength of steel." May we continue to be just that!

Before leaving our consideration of the function of change, I would like to underscore the fact that change is God's idea, his way of working his changeless, eternal purposes.

> God is the great change agent. He offers us purpose in life which is so stable and enduring it has stood the test of time. His enduring purpose for our world, for our shared life, and for us as individuals gives us a firm foundation for constructing our changing goals, activities, and relationships. God invites us to the new: new faith, new hope, and new love. New Life. He reveals his plans for us, and his plan is so good it creates dissatisfaction in us with life which misses the mark of his intentions. He holds out to us the better conditions of life lived in his Spirit and the ultimate gift of eternal life. Change. God offers us the possibility of renewing change—change which regenerates us and restores us to a right relationship with him, with each other, and with our universe.[10]

The Force of Change

Denomination renewal cannot come without planned change. We must honestly and openly identify the factors that hold us back from becoming what we ought to be—indeed what God wants us to be. We need to agree on being at our best what we have always been—a people united on mission. We need to acknowledge that which is changeless and those truths and values to which we are totally committed. Then we need to dismember that which is holding us back and carefully, with deep resolve, work together with God on the changes that bring about renewal. Our task is to acknowledge those things which are unchanging while addressing that which is dynamic.

Organization renewal bears a close kinship to spiritual renewal. The whole gospel is change-oriented, from the initial change of conversion through the continuing change of growth in grace. Perhaps we can visualize denomination renewal in steps similar to those we have undertaken in personal Christian pilgrimage.

What then are the steps we may take toward constructive, planned change? I suggest the following eight:

1. *Understand the current situation.* We need to recognize that the denomination is subject to what Kurt Lewin calls driving and restraining forces, which exist in any situation in which change is likely to occur. *"Driving forces* are those forces affecting a situation which are 'pushing' in a particular direction; they tend to initiate a change and keep it going. . . . *Restraining forces* are forces acting to restrain or decrease the driving forces. Apathy, hostility, and poor maintenance of equipment may be examples of restraining forces against increased production. Equilibrium is reached when the sum of the driving forces equals the sum of the restraining forces."[11]

What are the driving forces in our denomination today? What are the restraining forces? How shall we raise our level of denominational statesmanship and the impact we can have on a lost world through a careful, controlled increase in the driving forces and a proportionate decrease in restraining forces?

2. *Establish an initiating group.* Our Southern Baptist Convention leadership, once committed to denomination renewal, needs to identify and establish through appropriate and existing channels a group responsible for initiating the desired change. Significant grass-roots involvement is essential in implementing and sustaining any Bold Mission Thrust-type effort.

One feature of successful change is the involvement of those persons and organizations affected by the change at an early stage. How well are we doing this now in the denomination? It appears to me that an increasing number of Baptists and churches feel left out of the planning and decision-making processes of the denomination. Widespread involvement of persons at an early stage of planning helps to ensure that the plans won't have to be radically changed somewhere down the road. Such involvement will also lower the resistance to changes being implemented.

With this kind of early involvement, we can establish and maintain a relationship built around productive change.

3. *Create the climate for change.* At this step, the level of discontent with reality is raised and channeled into problem solving. Here we must be especially cautious. To raise the level of discontent with reality *without* channeling it into problem solving is to create utter chaos. For many of our people, this confusion and chaos aptly describes their response. Another way of expressing the creation of the climate for change is to catch a vision of the ideal and to "unfreeze" the current situation. One of the values of the present controversy in our midst is that we have an "unfrozen situation" to work with.

4. *Consider alternative courses of action.* We understand the problem; we have a group working diligently to create a climate for solution. Now, we review the options available to us based on a thorough and accurate diagnosis of the problem. As Edward Lindaman has said, "We contemplate not only *possible* options but also *preferred* options."[12]

Some courses of action would be anathema to Southern Baptists. Others would be bold, forward looking, and strategically powerful.

For example, suppose Southern Baptists decided that our business as a denomination is first and foremost to reach people for Jesus Christ and his churches. Just imagine what would happen if we sought to express this conviction by reaching for discipleship and membership *one tenth* of the population of the United States by AD 2000—26.7 million Southern Baptists! That *preferred option* would affect every component of our denomination, dominate the allocation of vast and growing resources, and require a quality of Christian discipleship much more representative of the New Testament era. (Ch. 9 deals with this course of action extensively.)

5. *Develop a supporting group.* In formulating strategy and tactics, the initiating group should be enlarged to include persons with specialized knowledge, groups with diverse expertise, and coalitions which need to be formed to produce the most lasting and far-reaching results. John Naisbitt's network concept would serve well our Baptist polity and propensity to cooperate.

6. *Implement the plan of action.* Once the supporting group is identified, they proceed according to clear assignment to implement the plan of action. They seek to reduce the restraining forces and intensify the driving forces in a carefully monitored effort. The implementers draw upon these five resources for this process: courage, skill, personnel, goodwill, and loyalty. By diligent and competent use of all the resources available to them, they change the situation, moving to a higher level—a level of renewal.

7. *Stabilize at the new and higher level.* Has renewal been achieved? Yes, but in a sense, it is a process without end. Here is the point at which review and evaluation are critical. This must take place before further adjustments in the plan are made. Once progress seems satisfactory, the situation which was "unfrozen" at point 3 is now frozen at this new, more vigorous and dynamic level.

The groups involved may now step aside and let the ongoing processes of the denomination operate at the heightened level of sensitivity and accomplishment.

In a sense, the dynamics of change are such that the process never ends. If denomination renewal is to continue, constant evaluation and readjustment must take place.

8. *Finally, bathe the whole change process in prayer.* Not a tacked-on prayer. Not just starting the proceedings with prayer and closing with prayer. But moving through the entire change process with all of our minds given to God for him to use them. Keeping our spirits attuned to the Holy Spirit—seeking to follow his leading.

In this chapter, I have not attempted to give solutions to specific problems we face but to encourage us to consider a change process that turns an enemy into an ally. This *blueprint* is based on the threefold reality that (1) change is inevitable and can be managed; (2) Southern Baptists are a great people capable of walking and working by *faith;* and, finally, (3) it is not the denomination that endures eternally but we seek a city whose builder and maker is God.

Notes

1. Lyle Schaller, *The Change Agent* (Nashville: Abingdon Press, 1972), p. 183.

2. John Naisbitt, *Megatrends* (New York: Warner Books, Inc., 1982), pp. 1-2.

3. Daniel Yankelovich, *New Rules* (New York: Random House, 1981), p. 5.

4. Ibid., p. 19.

5. Philip Lesly, *The People Factor* (Homewood, Illinois: Dow Jones-Irwin, 1974) pp. 36-37.

6. Elaine Dickson, *Say No, Say Yes to Change* (Nashville: Broadman Press, 1982), p. 18.

7. Lee Grossman, *The Change Agent* (New York: AMACOM, 1974), p. 4.

8. Alvin Toffler, *Future Shock* (New York: Bantam Books, Inc., 1970), p. 2.

9. Michael A. Berger, "Coping with Anarchy in Organizations," in *The 1981 Handbook for Group Facilitators* (San Diego: University Associates, Inc., 1981), pp. 135-37.

10. Dickson, pp. 28-29.

11. Paul Hersey and Kenneth H. Blanchard, "The Management of Change," *Training and Development Journal,* (June 1982), p. 84.

12. Edward Lindaman, *Thinking in the Future Tense* (Nashville: Broadman Press, 1978), p. 29.

8
Conflict Resolution

Challenge #8: As a people of God, let us acknowledge our differences, resolve our conflicts, and learn to live together in a fellowship of trust and strength.

Ephesians 4:31-32: Let all bitterness and wrath and anger and clamor and slander be put away from you, along with all malice. And be kind to one another, tender-hearted, forgiving each other, just as God in Christ also has forgiven you.

Organization Conflict: Conflict is universal in human affairs, but so are forces that mediate and resolve conflict. Organizations often face turbulent, ambiguous, and hostile environments containing forces which generate conflict. . . . Conflict goes with change. It is the price of change and an instigator of change. Conflict is generated in the reordering of interests affected by change . . . The fact that conflict may be beneficial or constructive does not preclude the possiblity of destructive conflict. Some conflicts are so severe, so long-lasting, that they drain off energy and resources that could be devoted to better use.

DALTON E. MCFARLAND[1]

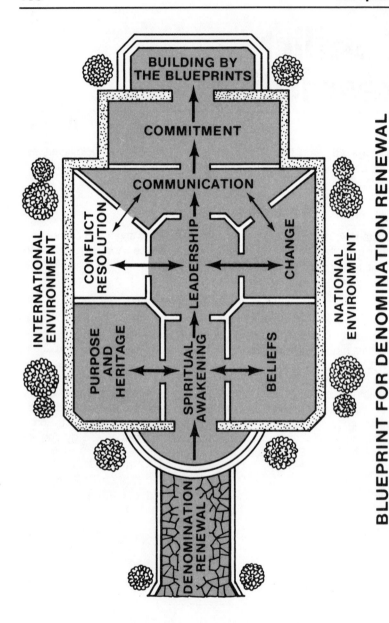

BLUEPRINT FOR DENOMINATION RENEWAL

Of conflict there seems to be no end, only more of the same. In the last chapter, I suggested the addition of *change* to any list of things inevitable, such as death and taxes. Now it's time to add another—*conflict*.

In February of 1983, I went before the trustees of the Baptist Sunday School Board for an interview and election as president. During the interview one trustee asked, "In working with Southern Baptists, the president of our Board sometimes receives criticism. How do you respond to criticism?"

"I don't like it!" My immediate response was slightly facetious but mostly honest. I added, "I don't like criticism, but I have learned that it is inevitable. Some of it is well-deserved and often it can be helpful. Even criticism that seems unfair can provide a learning experience that develops your determination to become your best. But you have to learn from criticism, then lay it aside and move on."

That just about describes my basic attitude toward conflict—personal or organizational. Conflict is normal, inevitable, can be helpful, might be destructive; but it must be dealt with, can't be avoided, and can be resolved.

In chapter 1, I set forth some problems among our Southern Baptist fellowship that many Baptists perceive. Also in that chapter, I set forth a guiding concept of this book that there are stages of denominational development and that at each stage of development there are issues to be resolved. It is my belief that a major dimension of our present struggle is that of change and conflict resolution. One of the most noticeable evidences of our need for denomination renewal is the content, diversity, and intensity of our problems and troubles.

The consequences of past Baptist conflicts have demonstrated that controversy is not always bad nor is it all bad. It can be a powerful stimulus for growth. On the other hand, it can have destructive power. It is most interesting, even encouraging, to me to view the Southern Baptist Time Line (see inside front cover) and to study the relationship between the major controversies of our Convention and its progress in growth. In spite of conflict, if not because of it, God has continued to give us a place of growing ministry.

In this present chapter on conflict resolution, I want to trace another important blueprint for denomination renewal. In considering this challenge, we will look at conflict—its reality, its roots, its resolution, and its renewing power.

The Reality of Conflict

No one can live long in the human family without experiencing conflict. We experience conflict within ourselves. There is conflict between persons in the family. Teachers and students have conflict. Employers and employees within an organization often disagree. Special-interest groups lobby against each other. And nations fight each other. Yes, even churches and denominations have problems with conflict. Conflict is as old as Adam and Eve and as recent as the front page of today's paper.

Conflict gets under our skin. Sometimes it goes as deep as our hearts. In the midst of conflict, faces get red, voices become harsh, blood pressures rise, pulses increase, breathing quickens, perspiration breaks out.

While conflict is something in which we find ourselves on a regular basis, none of us likes it. There are many ways we react to conflict. Sometimes

- We deny it.
- We fight back aggressively.
- We run from it.
- We fight back covertly.
- We give in to our opponent, hoping to stop the conflict.
- We confront the conflict, look at it, try to understand it, and give the most creative response possible.

Religious Conflict

Conflict is a part of everyday life. It is also a part of religious experience. There is some irony in this. Most religions offer approaches to salvation—the desire to be saved from many ills including conflict. But conflict becomes a part of religion. In fact, there are few conflicts so intense as religious conflicts.

Religious differences add fuel to many of the violent conflicts in the world today. People may do things in the name of God that they would never do otherwise.

Conflict Among Baptists

The present conflict among Southern Baptists isn't overtly violent. But there is conflict. And in it, we may not only be wasting time and energy but we may also be experiencing conflict that hinders our mission of sharing the saving power of Christ.

In 1984, Bob Hastings, editor of *The Illinois Baptist,* interviewed some fellow Baptists on their reaction to our religious conflict. Don Sharp, president of the Illinois Baptist State Association, gave the following response:

> When the unbeliever reads today's headlines, it crystallizes his opinion that being a Christian, or 'religious,' doesn't really change anything. It reinforces his belief that he knows many non-Christians who treat other people better than Christians do. Unfortunately, the entire history of the Christian church is replete with violence. So we send our mixed signals to the world, confusing those on the periphery. This is true, even when we as Christians get embroiled in non-violent controversy, each claiming to be 'right' to the exclusion of anyone else's opinion.[2]

The answer is not to deny conflict. Not to run from it. Conflict is a reality of human life. We must face that. In fact, one of our greatest witnesses may be in facing conflict where there are differences that are important and need to be dealt with. But *how* we argue with each other and *how* we cope with our conflicts may be one of the greatest witnesses to a world that is desperate to know that there is a better way to abundant life and trusting relationship.

Our own Southern Baptist history should encourage us to face the reality of our present conflict. We're in about the tenth major conflict we've been through as Southern Baptists. Two Baptist historians, Lynn E. May and Walter B. Shurden, have been most perceptive in pointing out the benefit to our life and growth of earlier conflicts.

In his preface to *Not a Silent People,* Walter B. Shurden tells about his wife's being taken aback when she saw the amount of conflict in Baptist churches. (Mrs. Shurden grew up in another denomination.)

> The thing that struck her was the amount of fussin' and fightin' that goes on there but to her it is a sign of life, of vitality, of concern. She declared on one occasion that she did not know that religious groups "cared enough to argue over anything." My response was if religious controversy is an index of how much people care, then Baptists care more then any group in the world.[3]

In the first volume of the *Encyclopedia of Southern Baptists* published in 1958, Lynn E. May wrote an article on the crises that Southern Baptists faced up to that time. May observed some common elements in each of these crises:

> First, there would be proposed a theory which was either an extreme conclusion drawn from a valid doctrine or a distorted position close enough to Baptist ideas to be attractive and far enough away to be corrupting. Many people would adopt this new theory, and there would be a division, often accompanied by heated controversy. Southern Baptists would then be forced to clarify or redefine the aspect of doctrine or polity in question. Dissident elements would withdraw, and Southern Baptists would be left reduced in numbers but committed more strongly than ever to their distinctive and newly understood position. Always their gain in understanding and commitment has more than compensated for their loss in numbers and has led to greater accomplishments than could have been achieved by the denomination as it existed before the crisis occurred.[4]

Conflict in Organizations

Those who have studied the nature and operation of organizations acknowledge the reality and nature of conflict.

Those of us who love our Baptist family need to understand our denomination as a large, complex spiritual-human-economic-missionary organization. We must also be honest about organizational conflict in our midst.

Let me present a brief analysis of the stages of conflict within our denomination. The framework for this analysis is adapted from L. R. Pondy's research as reported in "Organizational Conflict: Concepts in Models."[5]

Pondy has described conflict within an organization as a dynamic process between two or more individuals. According to Pondy, organizational conflict is neither good nor bad but must be evaluated in terms of function and dysfunction.

Pondy isolates five developmental stages of conflict in the following way:

1. Latent Conflict: The conditions of conflict may be summarized under three basic types:

   (1) Competition for scarce resources available within the denomination to get the job done causes conflict. An example of this is the allocation of funds by the local church, the state convention, or the Southern Baptist Convention.

   (2) Drives for autonomy cause conflict when one Baptist entity or person seeks to exercise power over another's province or activity.

   (3) The divergence of goals causes conflict when two or more Baptist entities must cooperate on some joint activity but are unable to reach a consensus.

2. Perceived Conflict: Conflict may be perceived at the cognitive level when no actual conditions of latent conflict exist. Latent conflict conditions may actually be present in the denomination without any of the participating Baptists per-

ceiving the conflict. This may explain some of our delayed reaction or stockpiling of conflicts until recent years.

3. Felt Conflict: A stage of the conflict episode beyond perception which includes tension and anxiety:

   (1) When the demands or expectations of the denomination are in conflict with and cause personal identity crisis of the individual or

   (2) When a Baptist's whole personality is tied up in the conflict episode of the denomination. This would include matters related to doctrinal positions, individual freedom, presidential elections, etc.

4. Manifest Conflict: One of the several varieties of behavorial conflict such as aggression or apathy, rebellion or rigid adherence, physical or verbal violence. At this stage conflict as such is not unintended but is deliberate and conscious. Such conflict among Baptists has most often taken the form of verbal abuse, knowingly blocking one another's goals, and/or noncooperative behavior.

5. Conflict Aftermath: Each of the five stages of conflict is one of a sequence in our Baptist denominational relationships. This stage called Conflict Aftermath may give us one of two possible legacies:

   (1) Genuine conflict resolution most often leads to satisfaction of a larger number of Baptist participants, more cooperation among individuals and Baptist entities, the expansion of available resources for kingdom purposes—in short, movement toward denomination renewal.

   (2) Suppressed Conflict may be more aggravated and the aftermath may explode into a new, more complex crisis.[6]

We have looked at the reality of conflict. It will help us understand the reality of conflict and enable us to be more effective in resolving conflict if we look at the roots of conflict.

The Roots of Conflict

Where does conflict begin? What are its roots? The answer lies deep in *human nature* (and in the nature of organizations as described). To be a finite creature made in the image of God is to be subject to conflict. Some may see conflict as only a result of sin, but even before Adam sinned, he had the capacity for choice. God told him and Eve not to eat of the tree of the knowledge of good and evil. Both Adam and Eve experienced conflict in deciding whether they should obey God or whether they should eat of the fruit. Conflict was rooted in human experience prior to the entry of sin into the world.

Jesus, who was without sin, experienced conflict. As a young boy, there was conflict with his parents that resulted from a misunderstanding. Just after his baptism and at the beginning of his public ministry, Jesus experienced great conflict when Satan tempted him. Early in his public ministry, Jesus was at odds with the religious leaders and they with him. This growing conflict was a road that led to his death on the cross. Although conflict has its roots apart from sin, there is no question but that sin has added a tragic dimension to conflict. But God's redeeming grace is sufficient for even the tragic dimension of conflict if we accept that grace.

If we look at how our children grow from infants, how they become adolescents, and then adults, we will see that conflict is a *developmental, normal, necessary part of life*. If children are ever going to be anything more than bundles of impulses that are expressed one after another, they must begin to say *no* to some impulses and *yes* to others. Their parents and society require that they begin to curb some of their impulses. This painful process of separation from parents creates conflict in the child and between the child and his parents. But human growth is possible only through such developmental conflicts.

The question is not whether there will be conflict. Human life as we know it isn't possible apart from conflict. The question is how we will understand the conflict and what we will do as we experience it.

Another root of conflict among people is *personality differences*. There are many ways that psychologists have divided up the human family into types. One of the ways we can be grouped is according to our dominant style of perceiving the world. Some people are strong in their ability to think. They are analytical. They seek to be as precise as possible in verbalizing reality as they experience it.

Other people are strongly intuitive. They like to deal with wholes rather than trying to divide wholes up into their component parts. Other persons are strong in experiencing reality through their emotions. Still others are heavily invested in perceiving reality through their senses.

Among devout Baptists, there are different ways of experiencing reality. Our difference with a fellow believer may not relate to important issues. It may have more to do with our diverse approaches to perception. You and I may prefer different approaches to worship, not so much because we disagree on our beliefs but because our dominant way of knowing is different.

Do not the deepest *roots of destructive conflict* thrive in the damp soil of hate, divisiveness of spirit, and diversity of purpose? Do they not spread out as they are watered by selfishness, conceit, and self-interest? And can these roots not be extracted by the application of the reconciling attitude that is part of the mind of Jesus Christ?

> If therefore there is any encouragement in Christ, if there is any consolation of love, if there is any fellowship of the Spirit, if any affection and compassion, make my joy complete by being of the same mind, maintaining the same love, united in spirit, intent on one purpose. Do nothing from selfishness or empty conceit, but with humility of mind let each of you regard one another as more important than himself; do not merely look out for your own personal interests, but also for the interests of others. Have this attitude in yourselves which was also in Christ Jesus (Phil. 2:1-5).

However, are not the deepest *roots of productive* conflict planted in the warm soil of high purpose, within a fellowship of profound trust, strong commitments, priorities, intention, and vigorous forward movement?

In an *organizational context,* McSwain and Treadwell identify four different sources of conflict: attitudes, substantive issues, emotions, and communication. Stemming from these sources, conflict moves through four steps to conclusion. These steps are:

(1) *Assumptions.* Those involved have certain opinions about how the matter began, the issues that are involved, how to approach the matter, and what would be to their own best interests with respect to resolution. These assumptions are sometimes confused with eternal principles.

(2) *Context.* Every conflict exists in a context. The inerrancy conflict in our denomination exists in a context of conservative belief about the Bible, believer's freedom, and denominational emphasis.

(3) *Events.* Many skirmishes in a conflict may occur before the conflict becomes public knowledge and property of the denomination. In the controversy over *The Message of Genesis,* for example, many actions on the part of the Sunday School Board trustees and Midwestern Baptist Theological Seminary trustees took place before two succeeding Southern Baptist Convention sessions dealt thoroughly and at length with the matter.[7]

(4) *Engagements.* This deals with the way people react to conflict events. We have already noted that some choose withdrawal. Others choose a fight response. How very important it is for Southern Baptists to let the mind and Spirit of Christ guide the events and engagements of conflict.

The Resolution of Conflict

Having looked at some of the roots of personal and organizational conflict, we are now better able to look at some approaches to the resolution of conflict. They take the form of biblical patterns, personal inventory, negotiations, problem-solving, de-escalation activities, and trusting participation.

Biblical Patterns

The first approach to resolution of conflict is to apply the power of faith in Christ to relationship behavior within the denomination. There are those all around us who do this beautifully as a consistent practice. Resolution of conflict among the people of God is both the expectation and the potential given to us from our Christian faith. A study of the biblical patterns, although not fully presented in this chapter, must include:

- *Confrontation:* "And if your brother sins, go and reprove him in private; if he listens to you, you have won your brother" (Matt. 18:15).
- *Counsel:* "But if he does not listen to you, take one or two more with you" (Matt. 18:16).
- *Church:* "And if he refuses to listen to them, tell it to the church" (Matt. 18:17).
- *Discipline:* "And if he refuses to listen even to the church, let him be to you as a Gentile and a tax-gatherer" (Matt. 18:17).
- *Judging:* "Do not judge lest you be judged. For in the way you judge, you will be judged; and by your standard of measure, it will be measured to you" (Matt. 7:1-2).
- *Confession:* "Therefore, confess your sins to one another, and pray for one another" (Jas. 5:16).
- *Concern for Others:* "Do not merely look out for your own personal interests, but also for the interests of others" (Phil. 2:4; see also Rom. 15:1-2).
- *Peacemakers:* "Blessed are the peacemakers, for they shall be called sons of God" (Matt. 5:9). "If possible, so far as it depends on you, be at peace with all men" (Rom. 12:18).
- *Humility:* "For everyone who exalts himself shall be humbled, and he who humbles himself shall be exalted." (Luke 14:11; see also Jas. 4:6-7; 1 Pet. 5:6-7; Rom. 12:3).

Encouraging counsel to the Southern Baptist family:

We need to hear and responsibly consider criticisms that come from within the denomination—insisting that these criticisms be without malice and affirming the merit of criticism given in love as essential to the correction of errors and the preservation of unity.
Ellis Bush, Exec. Dir.-Treas., Pennsylvania-South Jersey

We do have tensions—but tension is constructive. It pulls on us and we are being pulled back to some basics by these tensions. We look at ourselves and can be quite discouraged, but God has and is still using us.
Wayne Dehoney, President, SBC, 1965-1967

The number one priority in the lives of Christians is to love the Lord with all our hearts, souls, minds, and strength and our neighbors as ourselves.
Landrum P. Leavell, President, New Orleans Seminary

I would want every Southern Baptist to bear one another's burdens, and have a realistic view of ourselves (Gal. 6:1-4). Also, I would urge us to avoid speaking with bitterness, wrath, and anger. Rather let us build up the churches, be kind, and forgive those who have wronged us just as Christ forgave us (Eph. 4:29-32).
Frank Pollard, President, Golden Gate Seminary

Keep doing what we are doing—only better. We need to quit fussing and start working together.
Joe L. Ingram, Exec. Dir.-Treas., Oklahoma

Let us be slow to argue, quick to forgive, tolerant of others' beliefs, loyal to the Spirit of Christ.
R. M. Stephenson, Exec. Dir., Virginia

Where disagreement arises, let us listen and talk to one another in the acknowledged personal presence of God.
Robert M. Turner, Dir., Conference Center Division, BSSB

- *Forgiveness:* "For if you forgive men for their transgressions, your heavenly Father will also forgive you. But if you do not forgive men, then your Father will not forgive your transgressions" (Matt. 6:14-15; see also Matt. 18:21-22).
- *Reconciliation:* "Leave your offering there before the altar, and go your way; first be reconciled to your brother, and then come and present your offering" (Matt. 5:24).
- *Love:* "A new commandment I give to you, that you love one another, even as I have loved you, that you also love one another" (John 13:34; see also Matt. 5:43-44; Gal. 5:14).

Such biblical patterns should guide all of us in our Baptist family in all that we say, hear, believe, decide, and do. Our goal is not simply a trouble-free fellowship or an easy peace or a compromised position but a *practiced faith in Christ* in the midst of a redeemed and renewed fellowship.

Personal Inventory

The second approach to resolution of conflict is one that is rarely mentioned in the management literature on conflict. But the result of this approach is presupposed in other approaches to be presented in confronting conflict.

This action is to take a *personal inventory* by asking, *How am I contributing to this conflict? What is it in me or about my position that is making this conflict possible?* It usually takes two or more to have a conflict. If one of the parties to the conflict were different, there might not be a conflict. So it's worth asking the question, *What is it about me that is adding fuel to this conflict? How do I see my opponent? What is it about my opponent that bothers me?*

Let's take a case. I have a friend who considers himself very conservative in his beliefs. He sees himself as a fundamentalist. Those who differ with him are considered moderate, if not liberal. What is it about moderates that bothers him? How well does he know people whom he considers more liberal than he? Is there something about moderates that makes him afraid?

One of the fears we all have is dealing with people who are different from us. We fear that there may be some truth in their position. If we are somewhat comfortable in our present position, we fear the uncomfortable process of change which might be required if we understood another person's position better. A conservative may fear that the person more moderate might be right in some areas. The moderate may fear that the conservative might be right in some ways that would require some changes in his own life.

One of the common defenses we often use in maintaining our current position is to see in others undesirable qualities that we ourselves have. Perhaps a moderate has conservative tendencies which he fears since his dominant position in his life is to be open, not bound to tradition. Rather than recognizing this, he sees this conservatism in other people and he dislikes it because he dislikes it in himself. Or perhaps the conservative has some moderate tendencies which he fears. He doesn't face this but sees those who differ with him as being moderate. Thus the fight begins.

This same kind of thing happens in the area of ascribing motives. Those who consider themselves outside the establishment see the establishment as concerned primarily with protecting their own power base. Those in the establishment may see their critics as people who are primarily concerned about gaining power and control. It could be that both are overlooking their own concern with power and control and ascribing to others something that they need to face in themselves.

Taking a personal inventory can help a person see what's going on within and what he is bringing to the conflict. Recognizing one's own inner conflicts and one's own motivations can help one better see what is going on in the conflict. This is not as easy as it sounds. But it will improve our vision. This is exactly what Jesus commanded us to do when he said, "And why do you look at the speck that is in your brother's eye, but do not notice the log that is in your own eye? Or how can you say to your brother, 'Let me take the speck out of your eye,' and behold, the log is in your own eye? You hypocrite, first take the log out of your own eye, and then you will see clearly enough to take the speck out of your brother's eye" (Matt. 7:3-5).

Negotiation

Negotiation has been described as "a basic means of getting what you want from others."[8] For the Christian it is more than that. Fisher and Ury in *Getting to Yes* point out that principled negotiation is an honorable means of resolving conflict, "whether there is a prescribed ritual, as in collective bargaining, or an impromptu free-for-all, as in talking with hijackers."[9]

The skillful and principled negotiator looks for a way to get what he or she wants without causing the other party to feel that he or she has lost. In other words, a win-win result is preferable to a win-lose or, certainly, to a lose-win or a lose-lose outcome.

Herb Cohen could be considered a professional negotiator. In his book *You Can Negotiate Anything,* he emphasizes that the negotiator must be able to make his point and present his case without making a visceral opponent—an emotional enemy. This is accomplished, he says, by the following two rules:

1. Never forget the power of your attitude.
2. Never judge the actions and motives of others.

In the negotiation process, Cohen has a simple message: "You can get what you want if you recognize that each person is unique and that needs can be reconciled. At the same time never forget that most needs can be fulfilled by the way you act and behave."[10]

Perhaps the classical example of successful negotiation in early Southern Baptist life relates to the founding of The Sunday School Board. The committee formed for the purpose of making a recommendation asked the two strong leaders who had opposing views, J. M. Frost and J. B. Gambrell, to work out a solution. The committee believed that any agreement that these two spiritual giants with opposing convictions could reach would be highly satisfactory. The two men closed themselves in a hotel room, talked and prayed the matter through until they reached a compromise. In Frost's words,

> After much conferring together, and at the close of a conference which lasted practically all day, he (Gambrell) proposed to let me write the report and even name the location of the Board, provided he could write the closing paragraph. When the report was written, he added his words, they were accepted, provided he would let me add one sentence.[11]

Gambrell's last paragraph called for "fullest freedom of choice" for the churches while Frost's last sentence read, "But we would earnestly urge all brethren give to this Board a fair consideration, and in no case to obstruct it in the great work assigned to it by the Convention."

It fell, then, to the magnificent leadership of John A. Broadus on the Convention floor to lead those present to accept the report without divisive debate. "The spirit of controversy was muzzled, even as the spirit of the storm of Galilee was at the Master's word."[12]

We would do well to study this incident in depth as a model of negotiations for solving present-day conflicts.

In summary, "negotiation is a skill and an art. Settlements are negotiated because the settlement is beneficial to both sides. Skillful negotiators never lose sight of this certainty. If you analyze the facts as well as each side's needs and desires, you can then go after the solution that will benefit not only you but your adversary as well."[13] Southern Baptists would do well to remember how many of our practical positions are not ultimate and, therefore, are open to honest negotiation.

Problem-solving

Problem-solving is another classic approach to conflict resolution. There are many models, all of which have some variation on a common theme. One such model has six steps in the process:
   1. Identify and define the problem.

2. Generate alternative solutions.
3. Evaluate the alternative solutions.
4. Make the decision.
5. Implement the decision.
6. Follow up to evaluate the situation.[14]

In our complex information society, we need in great abundance the gift of administration expressed in the area of problem-solving. How true this is of our denomination:

> Problem-solving is the elixir of management skills. It is the skill that can help to identify the other skills that need improvement. It is the continuous skill of the roles of relationship builder, communicator, and decision-maker. The tasks of authentic spiritual direction, efficient organization, and effective leadership in the building and maintaining of psychological contracts and faithful covenant are constant and complex. Count on things going wrong, mistakes happening, and people becoming upset. In this management of ministry such mistakes are opportunities for increased communication, the improvement of our capacities to solve problems, and the clarification of our corporate gifts.[15]

Conflict De-escalation

Another form of conflict resolution is de-escalation. This is very similar to negotiation. The steps as listed by Speed Leas are:

1. Establish boundaries.
2. Structure the process.
3. Search together for common goals.
4. Respond to threats with descriptions and statements of your position, not threats.
5. Bring in a third party.[16]

Conflict, Leas believes, "is more than a function of interpersonal dynamics. Much of what shapes conflict and starts it in the first place has to do with factors that are beyond the interaction of individual personalities. Some conflict is structured into the fabric of an organization."[17] Is not some conflict structured into the fabric of our denomination? The conflict has been de-escalated by the approach of some to be open, to listen, to communicate, and to get people of opposing viewpoints together.

Trusting Participation

The final approach that seems particularly appropriate to our concern is that to which Wayne Oates alludes in *Christ and Self-hood*. He cites two foundations identified by Kurt Lewin for wholehearted individual action within a given group. These are:

> belief that the group is going in the right direction and second, primary trust in the leader of the group. These two foundations provide a group atmosphere of confidence and trust. The early church was able to resolve conflict of direction through the tutelage of the Holy Spirit in that they did not move upon the political idea of "the majority rule," but upon the firm intention to seek the gladness and singleness of heart of the Holy Spirit.[18]

Lewin also observed that *"certainty of belongingness* provides the basis for reconciliation within a group. The certainty of belongingness depends on the commitment of individuals to the directions of the group and the durability of the covenant that binds them together."[19]

Renewal Through Conflict

As we consider specific ways in which we might approach resolving denominational conflict, we cannot help but observe that the single most important factor is the spirit in which we undertake the task. We need a renewal of spirit in God's people in the midst of conflict. James L. Sullivan reminds us:

> In the end, polity is asking the question, How does God want Southern Baptists to do the job that is ours? Then, we are to relate ourselves in the way we feel his Book has revealed and his Spirit leads. With total abandonment, we can then surge forward. This is the Spirit that has brought us thus far. This is the Spirit that will lead us on.[20]

Political scientist James David Barber in *The Presidential Character* observes three recurring themes in American life—conflict, conciliation, and consensus. Are these traits of spirit not also needed among those who would lead the voluntary participation of millions of Southern Baptists?

Denomination renewal through conflict resolution will require disciplined, consistent action among Southern Baptists. We can do it. We have before. If we are to make a major contribution to the world as we move toward AD 2000, literally thousands of our people must act in trusting consensus. How can we behave in such a way that we resolve conflict constructively?

1. We must acknowledge openly and honestly without fear or discouragement that there are problems, differences, and conflicts among us.

2. We must as readily admit that there are by the grace of God and the good will of Baptist people solutions to be found and that we passionately seek them.

3. We must approach all conflict resolution according to the biblical patterns built around the love commandment—there must be love in a nonjudgmental spirit.

4. We must take a personal inventory, knowing what we believe, what positions are based soundly on biblical authority, and what should be open to counsel and change among the larger fellowship of believers.

5. We must seek to know and understand the beliefs and positions of our brethren from dependable sources and not from careless hearsay—we must cease to attack each other's motives.

6. We must be open to negotiation in good faith when the conflict is an open area of diverse positions held by other knowledgeable, devout Baptists.

7. We must engage in thoughtful, logical, problem solving and decision making based on facts, information, alternatives, feedback, and broad participation.

8. We must seek to build concensus among Southern Baptists

based on broad concerns, basic commitments, and conciliatory spirit rather than polarization and party spirit.

9. We must not try to resolve every conflict that comes along, lest we spend all our time separating the chaff from the wheat rather than working diligently in the fields of him who is the Lord of the harvest.

10. We must do all in a spirit of prayer to God, trust in his providential care, and dependence on his Spirit to guide us in our life together and our effort in all conflict resolution. In the words of Wayne Oates:

> The crucial work of the Holy Spirit in both individual and social conflict is the refinement of the motives of men, assaying the dross in clarifying the adulteration or wholeness of the decisions springing from these motives. The patient process of testing and refinement *is* the meaning of conflict, and the revelation of a wholehearted direction of united faith in the bonds of peace *is* the resolution. Through the resolution the growth takes place and the community is "built up" and "edified in love."[21]

Southern Baptists are a great people! We are well able to accept this challenge and act upon it to the glory of our sovereign Lord.

Notes

1. Dalton E. McFarland, *Management Foundations and Practices* (New York: Macmillan Publishing Co., Inc., 1979), pp. 404, 408.
2. Don Sharp as quoted by Bob Hastings in *The Illinois Baptist* (February 15, 1984), p. 4.
3. Walter B. Shurden, *Not a Silent People* (Nashville: Broadman Press, 1972), p. vii.
4. Lynn E. May, "Crises, Southern Baptist," *Encyclopedia of Southern Baptists,* Vol. 1 (Nashville: Broadman Press, 1958), p. 333.
5. L. R. Pondy, "Organizational Conflict: Concepts in Models," *Management of Change and Conflict* (Baltimore: Penguin Books, 1972), pp. 359-380.
6. Ibid.
7. Shurden, pp. 104 *ff.*
8. Roger Fisher and William Ury, *Getting to Yes* (New York: Penguin Books, 1983), p. xi.

9. Ibid.

10. Quoted in *Nation's Business* (May 1981), p. 90.

11. Robert A. Baker, *The Story of the Sunday School Board* (Nashville: Broadman Press, 1966), p. 43.

12. Ibid., p. 45.

13. *Soundview Executive Book Summaries,* Vol. 4, No. 6, Part 1, June 1982, p. 3.

14. *Soundview Executive Book Summaries,* Vol. 1, No. 16, 1979, p. 2.

15. James D. Anderson and Ezra Earl Jones. *The Management of Ministry* (New York: Harper & Row Publishers, Inc., 1978), p. 181.

16. Speed B. Leas, *Leadership and Conflict* (Nashville: Abingdon Press, 1982), p. 29.

17. Ibid., p. 87.

18. Wayne Oates, *Christ and Selfhood* (New York: Association Press, 1961), p. 149.

19. Ibid.

20. James L. Sullivan, *Rope of Sand with Strength of Steel* (Nashville: Convention Press, 1974), p. 129.

21. Oates, p. 152.

9
Commitment to Action

Challenge #9: As a people of God, let us hear and respond to the claims of Christ in such a way that individually as believers and corporately as a denomination we commit ourselves to concerted action to bring the peoples of this nation and of our world to salvation in Christ and fellowship in his church.

Romans 12:1-2: I urge you, therefore, brethren, by the mercies of God, to present [commit] your bodies a living and holy sacrifice, acceptable to God, which is your spiritual service of worship. And do not be conformed to this world, but be transformed by the renewing power of your mind, that you may prove what the will of God is, that which is good and acceptable and perfect.

Necessity of Commitment: We have reason to believe that civilization cannot be redeemed without the church as a redemptive society, but the disturbing thought, which must always be matched with this one, is that the church as we know it is not now good enough to fulfill its redemptive function. . . . The movement we need is a movement in depth, and if it is deep enough the problem of unity will take care of itself. . . . We could stand division if we had genuine commitment to Christ and his cause.

ELTON TRUEBLOOD[1]

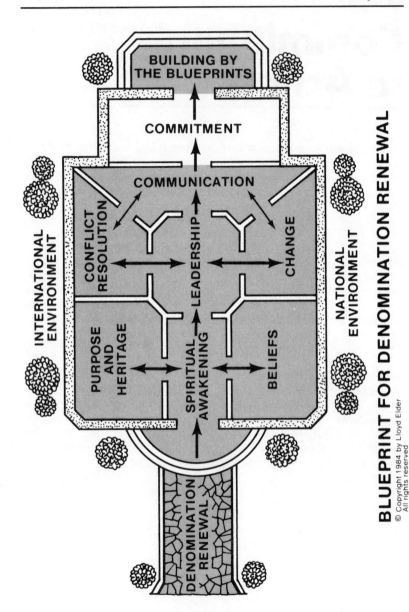

BUILDING BY
THE BLUEPRINTS

COMMITMENT

COMMUNICATION

CONFLICT RESOLUTION

CHANGE

LEADERSHIP

INTERNATIONAL ENVIRONMENT

NATIONAL ENVIRONMENT

PURPOSE AND HERITAGE

SPIRITUAL AWAKENING

BELIEFS

DENOMINATION RENEWAL

BLUEPRINT FOR DENOMINATION RENEWAL

As I sat down to write this chapter on commitment, my mind went back more than two decades. I was reminded of some experiences that were crucial in shaping me as a Christian, a Southern Baptist, and a pastor.

In 1961 I was serving as pastor in a small town. One of my great concerns was that our little congregation overcome some rather overwhelming odds and keep growing in ministry.

I had just completed my master's degree in the seminary and had enrolled for doctoral studies. During that time, Elton Trueblood came out with his seminal book *The Company of the Committed.* That book was both instructive and inspirational to me.

Out of that matrix—pastoring a small congregation, ongoing theological studies, personal aspirations, and Trueblood's book— there grew a longing that our Baptist churches would indeed be both redeemed and redemptive communities of faith. I had a strong desire we would make a radical commitment to be the missionary force in the total society as our Lord intended.

The years have come and gone, and that longing has never been fully realized. Neither has it been abandoned. I am still struggling with commitment at both the personal and denominational levels.

Commitment to action is a challenge to us as a people of God to hear and respond to the claims of Christ in such a way that individually as believers and corporately as a denomination we will commit ourselves to concerted action to bring the peoples of our nation and of our world to salvation in Christ and fellowship in his church. In the present chapter, I should like to begin by looking at the nature of commitment. In doing so, I shall draw on biblical examples and contemporary perspectives on the concept of commitment. I shall then sketch a picture of what might happen by the year 2000 if we as a people of God wholeheartedly give ourselves to him to be used in his purposes.

A Biblical Understanding

Basic Meanings

Words like *commit* and *commitment* come alive with vibrant meaning when they are defined. Commitment means:

- The act of entrusting, of giving in trust, of keeping in trust, of putting someone in charge, of transferring.
- The act of pledging, or promising to do something, an open declaration committing oneself to a course of action.
- The act of doing something or performing a deed or duty.
- The accomplishment of an act.

The most common New Testament Greek word for *commit* means to place beside, to set before, to put alongside. It is translated accurately in various contexts, as *commit, act, do, commend, present, set before, entrust, pledge, bind.*

The God of Abraham, Isaac, and Jacob—the God and Father of our Lord Jesus Christ—is a covenant God. He makes commitments to his people, and he looks for commitment from his people. The covenant God and his relationship to his covenant people is a unifying theme of biblical revelation.

Biblical Concepts

Commitment as an essential element in life is found throughout the biblical witness, far beyond the use of the word itself. It touches upon every dimension of the claims of Christ on the believer's life:

"Take up your cross and follow me" (Matt. 16:24).

"Seek first the kingdom of God and his righteousness" (Matt. 6:33).

"Lay up for yourselves treasures in heaven" (Matt. 6:20).

"I press toward the mark of the prize of the high calling" (Phil. 3:14).

"Go therefore and make disciples of all nations" (Matt. 28:19).

"And from everyone who has been given much shall much be required" (Luke 12:48).

"And He has committed unto us the word of reconciliation" (2 Cor. 5:19).

"And now I commit you to God and to the word of his grace" (Acts 20:32).

Any interest we as Southern Baptists have in denomination renewal and its expression in action must continually be rooted in the call and claims of the gospel. For in the death of Christ and his resurrection, we see how radical a commitment God has made to his people. What a pledge! Moreover, our actions must be rooted in the coming of the Holy Spirit at Pentecost. The Holy Spirit is God's commitment to us—his down payment of our total and final redemption. It is often said that we can't outgive God. Neither can we outcommit him. Our commitment will likely be as strong as our realization of the total commitment which God has made to us.

How do our commitments as Christians relate to our understanding and realization of God's commitment to us? There seems to be deep within all of us a false belief that we can save ourselves. It is easy to confess with our mouths that we are saved by grace. But often there persists the belief that our being accepted and loved by God depends on how much we are doing for God and how many overt sins we are refraining from. This kind of attitude does not allow persons to face their humanity and sinfulness. Not facing this leaves persons in a state of self-deception, contentiousness with other people, and defeat.

If my righteousness depends only on God's grace rather than on righteousness in myself, then I can progressively face my own humanity—sinfulness and all—knowing that my righteousness, my worth, my being loved, does not depend on anything in me. Commitment is a bridge to God's saving act on our behalf.

Profile of Commitment

Looking at Simon Peter's development from the point of view of commitment can be instructive.

In Luke's Gospel, the first picture we see of Peter is of a man who was convicted of his sinfulness in the presence of Jesus. But he responded to Jesus' invitation to follow him and be a disciple. As Jesus was on his way to Jerusalem for the last time, Peter reminded Jesus of the fact that he and others had left their homes to follow Jesus. The further Peter went with Jesus the more concerned he became about where it was all going to end—about what the payoff was going to be. Jesus assured Peter that those who had left all to follow him would be abundantly rewarded, not only in this present world but in the age to come.

For a brief moment Peter was strengthened. They went on to Jerusalem. But then Peter's commitment broke down during Jesus' questioning at the house of the high priest. The servant girl tried to link Peter with the controversial Galilean. Three times Peter denied the One to whom he was so strongly committed.

If, in the dark hours between Jesus' death and resurrection, Peter recalled the words of Jesus about his disciples being abundantly rewarded both in the present and the future world, he must have been greatly puzzled about the meaning of this saying.

The One to whom Peter had given his strongest commitment was dead. But not for long. In his resurrected glory, Christ made a special point to restore this disciple. These experiences transformed Simon Peter. Even though he realized that in his own power he had not been able to keep his commitment to the end, Peter had seen the radical nature of his sin and weakness. But more important, he experienced a forgiveness, a love, a worth, a righteousness that did not depend on his own ability.

Peter's center of allegiance was transferred from his own weak self—from his strong will, his good intentions, his dogged determination—to his Lord whose faithfulness was not diminished by Peter's weakness and failure.

It is that enduring love of Christ, that unfailing commitment of Christ to his people, that is the rock on which the church is built. Those who have been along the same path as Peter know they can rejoice not because they have strong willpower or because they are so effective in kingdom work. They rejoice because their names are written in heaven. They realize that nothing in all of creation can separate them from the love of God in Christ Jesus our Lord. Through experiences of this kind, they have learned what Jesus meant when he said that even the gates of hell cannot stand against the church.

This profile of Simon Peter lets us see several truths within the biblical understanding of commitment. The following insights about commitment are in harmony with those truths and are based on studies of both individuals and organizations.

The Human Side

Southern Baptists searching for widespread, ever-deepening commitment to the purposes of God will do well to consider just how commitment actually touches the human side of believers and of those whom we are seeking to reach. Let us now examine the human side of commitment.

Personal Commitment

Commitment looked at from the human side involves basic elements of life: attitudes, beliefs, effort, decisions, freedom, and behavior.

Charles A. Kiesler, a social psychologist, has reported his research in this area in a helpful book, *The Psychology of Commitment.*[2] The following sketch of the human side of individual commitment draws from that research.

Pledging is the dictionary meaning of the word *commitment.* Pledging is the binding of an individual to behavioral acts. Personal commitment is dedication to the completion of a line of action.

Attitudes and beliefs, that is, certain regularities of an individual's thoughts and feelings guide behavior on a day-to-day basis in a somewhat predictable response.

Effort is central to commitment and has a dramatic influence on behavior. It serves as a valid link between attitudes and behavior.

Decision is an act of commitment. A person is committed when he has decided to do or not to do a certain thing when he chooses one alternative and rejects others.

Freedom, or one's perception of freedom of choice, is a central feature of any understanding of personal commitment. Commitment is one's taking responsibility for one's own behavior.

Behavior, or action, is the truest expression of commitment. Through behavior one is committed. Attitudes are often fluid, beliefs may be denied, decisions may waver, but explicit behavior stands like a pillar of commitment, an irrevocable decision cast into living experience.

These critical elements of commitment from a strictly human dimension have a direct bearing on the effectiveness of our authentic efforts to get hosts of Southern Baptists committed to Bold Mission Thrust. But let us explore still other significant human elements related to commitment.

Human Needs

Commitment is related to motivation, and motivation is related to the drive to satisfy unmet human needs.

In the work of Christ, we have often looked at fellow Christians as purely spiritual beings. This is unrealistic. When persons are converted to Christ, they are still human beings. I continue to have a growing sense of wonder at the mysterious way in which God uses human beings in his purposes. He is able to take human needs and use them in the process of sanctification and in bringing us together as co-workers with him.

Dr. Abraham Maslow[3] has rendered a great service to students of human behavior by showing the range of needs that humans have:

1. Physiological needs: air, water, food, shelter, sleep, sex.
2. Basic needs for security and safety.
3. Social needs for affection, belonging, achievement, and recognition.
4. Ego needs for identity, self-esteem, and esteem by others.
5. Self-actualization needs, such as the need for meaning, self-sufficiency, simplicity, justice, truth, creativity, autonomy, individuality.

It is Maslow's contention that needs at a lower level must be satisfied before people can begin satisfying needs at a higher level. I think there is some truth to this. When persons are starving for food, they're not likely to be very concerned about self-actualization or creativity. When persons are physically ill, their first priority is to get well and then to move on with fulfilling other needs.

However, in my estimation, Victor Frankl has put his finger on humanity's *basic need.* That is the need for purpose and meaning in life. Frankl came to this discovery as an inmate in a Nazi concentration camp. Here he found that meaning could be found in three ways: (1) by doing a deed; (2) by experiencing a value, the highest of which is love; and (3) by suffering bravely.

It is almost certain that Frankl and others in concentration camps did not have a lot of their lower level needs met. They discovered that, with meaning found in one or more of the three ways that Frankl suggested, life was worth living even in a concentration camp.

Southern Baptists long to be the agents of reconciliation which God uses to bring the good news of redemption in Christ to a hurting, sinful, broken world. Before that can happen, we must recognize our own humanity and the humanity of our fellow Christians we wish to encourage and to call to join us in the task of bringing persons to God through Christ.

Human Rewards

Commitment is related to motivation expressed in a system described as intrinsic and extrinsic rewards. Let us review the implications of such rewards.

Human motivation is significantly affected by intrinsic rewards: those that originate within and are felt within a person. These include one's sense of achievement and accomplishment. A sense of self-esteem is an intrinsic reward and an important motivator. A sense of achievement, accomplishment, and self-esteem are rewards that satisfy the need for being responsible, autonomous, and challenged.

If Southern Baptists were to act on this and track the wisdom of the excellent companies and the wisdom of Christian motivation, we would seek to create an environment of intrinsic rewards for a larger number of Baptists. We would do more to support both personal development and development of skills for ministry, rewarding high performance, creativity, innovation, and autonomous responsibility. Intrinsic reward would fuel commitment.

Human motivation also includes extrinsic rewards. In the work setting, these rewards are external to the job itself. They are given by the business or organization to the individual in the form of pay, promotion, benefits, praise, tenure, status symbols, improved working conditions, equipment and facilities, and opportunities to relate to co-workers.

Our denominational reward system should be such that we reward and give recognition to (1) those who follow the call to difficult places of ministry such as new work areas or foreign missions and (2) those who render excellent service to the denomination through an association, a state Baptist convention or to a board, agency or institution of the Southern Baptist Convention. Excellence in ministry does not always bring with it results that are immediate and highly visible.

Self Interest

Commitment is a noble human capacity and powerful force

but may be too narrowly focused on self-interest or unworthy interests.

Persons can commit themselves to people who are not worthy of commitment. People can make commitments to organizations, causes, and nations whose courses are destructive and harmful. Often one sees some of the strongest commitments made to persons, causes, and actions that are not worthy of such commitment. We need to make our commitments with our eyes open, realizing that total commitment, ultimate commitment, belongs only to the Lord. Our commitments to finite persons and causes should be made only after careful thought and within the context of God's will.

In his book *New Rules,* Daniel Yankelovich has observed that we have lived through a period of ten or fifteen years when the notion of commitment has been unpopular. Commitment has been seen as something which restricts a person's freedom.

In his analysis of our contemporary American culture, Yankelovich sees the search for self-fulfillment as being a reaction to what he calls "the giving/getting compact."[4]

The giving/getting compact is really a summary of the American dream: "I give hard work, loyalty, and steadfastness. I swallow my frustrations and suppress my impulse to do what I would enjoy, and do what is expected of me instead. I do not put myself first; I put the needs of others ahead of my own. I give a lot, but what I get in return is worth it."[5]

There is a form of commitment in this giving/getting compact. One of the problems with this commitment is that it may be too narrow and that the person making it may not be as conscious as he should be about what he is committing himself to.

The reaction against the giving/getting compact involves a commitment primarily to oneself. The commitment is to discover one's needs and wants and to do whatever one can to meet those needs. This attitude is the me-first approach to life which has been so prevalent in the last few years. Both this reaction and the attitude and position against which it is reacting are too narrow. A person who blindly commits himself to another person, institution, or society in exchange for being cared for is not living out the freedom God has given him. On the other hand, the person who turns in on himself, whose primary commitment is to discover his own needs and meet those needs, cuts himself off from the Lord and other relationships through which his life would be most fulfilled. Yankelovich has observed that this is a paradox. This paradox was observed by our Lord when he said that the person who would find his life must first lose it.

This was the experience of the disciples whose commitment was based more on the Lord's strong commitment to them than on their power to commit themselves to him. These people centered their lives in a transcendent source—the risen Lord.

Commitment Ethic

Commitment in our American society needs to move away from commitment to mere self-interest toward an ethically grounded self-fulfillment that links the individual to society.

The contemporary understanding of commitment is enriched by the section on "Toward an Ethic of Commitment" in Yankelovich's book *New Rules.* Yankelovich suggests that there are two distinct steps required to develop a new, viable social ethic of commitment that binds the individual to society:

1. A change from the present strategies of fulfillment based on either the work ethic of self-denial or the hedonistic ethic of duty to self. The psychology of affluence and the me-first outlook have to go on the junk heap. The new ethic of self-fulfillment requires commitment that endures over a long period of time and that can be realized through a web of shared meanings that transcend the self viewed as an isolated physical object.

2. The second large step requires that people receive clear and distinct signals from the larger society: from political leadership, the mass media, institutional leadership, business, religion, education, labor, artists, scientists, the intellectual community, and

from the informal interchange of family and friends. The signals must permit people to understand how they can link their personal aspirations to the new realities of our society.[6]

This concept of a socially responsible individual ethic of commitment has its own dramatic implications for Southern Baptist life. It also builds a bridge toward the human side of commitment that can and must be shaped as part of our commitment to the kingdom of Christ.

Shaping Commitment

Commitment as one of our highest human capacities can be strengthened, can resist attack, can even be brought to higher levels.

Let us first look at how commitment can be strengthened. On the outskirts of Jerusalem, Peter reminded Jesus that he had left everything for Jesus—as if to ask what would be the return on this investment. Jesus answered that there would be a reward. This probably had a temporary strengthening effect on Peter's wavering commitment.

That commitment can be strengthened has been observed by Charles A. Kiesler. He has hypothesized that one can increase the degree of commitment by increasing the following variables:

- the explicitness of the act, how public or otherwise unambiguous the act was;
- the importance of the act;
- the degree of the irrevocability of the act;
- the number of acts performed by the subject; and
- the degree of volition perceived by the person in performing the act.[7]

We can see how these various factors work in strengthening commitment in such acts as marriage, public profession of faith in Christ, and by baptism.

Peter's confession at Caesarea Philippi that Jesus was the Christ, the Son of the Living God, was an explicit act. It was made in the presence of other disciples. This kind of public act would have a strengthening effect on Peter's commitment to Christ. Although Peter's insight was not of human origin, his expression of the insight in the company of other disciples strengthened his degree of commitment to the Lord.

When an attack on a committed person is not strong enough to drive the person from his commitment, he resorts to extreme behavior in defense of his commitment. This can be seen in the arrest of Jesus when one of Jesus' followers drew his sword and cut off the ear of the high priest's servant. This human tendency to strengthen one's commitment in the face of attack can be seen in the escalation of conflict.

For example, Saul of Tarsus saw the growth of the early church as an attack on the religion of his fathers. His behavior became extreme. His extreme behavior was matched by the early Christians in their willingness to suffer and even die for the sake of Christ. In Stephen's suffering, Paul saw a different quality of commitment than he had. Paul's seeing Stephen's commitment to Christ was a memory God used to bring Paul to a right understanding of who Jesus was.

Not only can commitment be strengthened but it can also be brought to a higher level. There is no question but that Simon Peter was as committed to his Lord as any human being could be. His denial simply shows the weakness and inability of human nature. Commitment that is only self-relying may be strong, but it is brittle. This kind of commitment is a dogged determination to hang on as long as one can. We see a different quality, a different kind of commitment, by the apostles on the other side of the resurrection and especially after Pentecost. They discovered that they didn't have to hold on so hard. They found themselves in strong, loving, gracious hands.

Their previous stance reminds me of the elderly man who was flying on an airplane for the first time. When he arrived at his destination, his son met him at the airport and asked, "Well Dad, how was the flight?" "Oh, it was just fine," he replied, "but I never fully put my weight down."

Encouraging counsel to the Southern Baptist family:

Let us pour our energies into winning the lost to Christ.
W. A. Criswell, President, SBC, 1969-1971

What unites us is more important than what divides us: namely, commitment to Christ. Heresy is bad, and it is also bad to hold sound theology and fail to have a Christlike love.
Johnnie C. Godwin, Dir., Holman Division, BSSB

"Let the church be the church." Without the commitment to evangelism based on the Word of God, the church cannot be the church.
Robert D. Hughes, Exec. Dir.-Treas., California

Each of us should be committed to seeing that every dollar spent by our agency was done so with the thought that it was absolutely necessary in the implementation of our purpose.
Hollis E. Johnson, III, Exec. Sec.-Treas., Southern Baptist Foundation

As Southern Baptists, we have the potential and resources to fulfill the mandate of our Lord. But God and the world still await the total commitment of our people.
Dan H. Kong, Exec. Dir., Hawaii

Let us commit ourselves to family worship, a family plan of stewardship, and a family plan of recreation.
Louie D. Newton, President, SBC, 1947-1949

Renew our commitment to our historic role as a people on mission and increase our missionary efforts.
Cecil A. Ray, National Dir., Planned Growth in Giving

With unexcelled resources in people, excellent printed helps, well-defined organization, we could win the world in this generation. Unity in our diversity is essential if we are to meet the challenge.
Carolyn Weatherford, Exec. Dir., WMU

The quality of our commitment changes when we come to recognize that our weight is already fully in God's hands. We might as well relax.

Dogged determination did not turn the pagan first-century world upside down. Men and women with wills of steel did not. But men and women who had become convinced beyond any doubt that Jesus was alive in their midst turned the world upside down. They believed that God was for them, that God was with them, that all of their enemies—even death—could not separate them from God, his love, and his purpose.

These were the people who spread the loving flame of the good news throughout the pagan world. They were human. They had disagreements. They were sinners. But they knew that they were forgiven. They were free to accept themselves as human, earthy vessels. They knew that no one—not even the accuser Satan—could bring a charge against them.

An Organizational View

Let us now move to the next step in our call for commitment—to our denominational missionary enterprises. In doing so, we move from the personal level to the consideration of *commitment to an organization*. It is one thing for Southern Baptists to have a personal commitment to Christ as Savior and Lord. But it may be quite another for that one Baptist and millions of other Baptists to be actively committed to the Bold Mission Thrust efforts of the Southern Baptist denomination. How do we get at that?

Personal Dimensions

Commitment to an organization, such as our denomination, is only given by large numbers of Southern Baptists if our denomination and all its components take seriously the foregoing biblical and personal dimensions of commitment. Treating with integrity the human side of commitment is absolutely essential if the denomination is to receive the long-term, productive, freely given commitment of its constituency. *People matter!* Of all organizations, our great denomination must seek to elicit genuine commitment rather than promote or manipulate superficial response. In the truest sense of the word, only individuals commit—not organizations or denominations.

Organizational Commitment

The concept of commitment to an organization has received increasing attention in research and practice in recent years. "Specifically, organizational commitment is viewed as the relative strength of an individual's identification with and involvement in a particular organization, as well as the willingness to exert effort and remain in the organization."[8] In a study on commitment to organizations, Kenneth Ferris and Nissim Aranya report two scales that have been used to measure commitment to an organization. They identify five different variables that have significance for our denomination as an organization. On this view, commitment is expressed as:

1. *identification* with the organization, a strong belief in and acceptance of its goals and values which form the basis for attachment to the organization;
2. *involvement* in the organizational work role, assessing the strength of attachment to the organization;
3. *loyalty,* warm affective regard for the organization;
4. *effort,* a willingness to exert considerable effort on behalf of the organization in order to achieve its goals; and
5. *membership,* a strong desire or willingness to remain in the organization and to facilitate its goals.

Practically speaking, business enterprises have been keenly interested in the relationship of commitment as a potential determinant to the employee who accepts employment, shows up for work (absenteeism), performs the tasks, and continues employment (turnover). And just as practically speaking, the denomination must be vitally interested in commitment as a determinant for (1) membership in the denomination, (2) involvement and performance in the work of Southern Baptists, and (3) continued participation over the years.

Results: Excellence

Excellent organizations are those that are able to inspire commitments from their employees. I have already mentioned the fact that social scientists have created instruments that can measure employees' degree of commitment to an organization. Beyond these precise measures of commitment, degree of commitment can be measured by the excellent results of the organization over a long period of time. It can also be seen on the faces of employees.

In their influential book *In Search of Excellence,* Peters and Waterman have shown that the excellent companies in the United States today are marked by commitment and enthusiasm on the part of their employees. These companies are both people-centered and results-oriented. They show an acceptance of human beings as they are, in all their strengths and weaknesses. By understanding their employees' needs and wants, these companies are able to inspire both commitment and creativity that play vital parts in the results they achieve.[9]

But understanding persons' needs and motives is not enough. Knowing these can lead to manipulation rather than life-giving motivation. We can apply the same test that we used in chapter 5 concerning servant leadership. Do the persons in the organization increase in well-being, or are their motives and needs simply exploited? Under a servant leader, human needs and motivations will be understood, but they will be engaged to promote not only results for the organization but the health, growth, and fulfillment of the people involved.

In his book *MBO for Non-Profit Organizations,* Dale McConkey presents a concept of "renewal by objectives."[10] He reports that study after study has demonstrated that persons will not be committed to helping achieve results unless they have had a voice in determining what the result will be. Conversely, people

will be more motivated to work for the success of a project if they
have had a part in developing it.

Renewal by objectives requires active involvement and participation by all members of a church. The pastor, the elected
leaders, and the congregation must be actively involved in fur-
thering the church's work.

High commitment and high motivation usually go hand in
hand. They depend on the degree to which a person believes this
is his or her project—the degree to which he or she owns it.

The late Douglas McGregor, one of the most respected behavioral scientists of this century, helped me to understand the
need for blending the efforts and interests of the individual
(church member) with those of the organization (the denomination).

It is possible to satisfy the self-actualization needs of persons
and at the same time the organizational objectives of the denomination. This has important implications for our goal of sharing the gospel with the world by AD 2000.

Before sketching a dream of what Southern Baptists could be
by AD 2000, I would like to share with you a sevenfold commitment I am making while in the process of this writing.

A Personal Commitment

In recent months many experiences, studies, and influences
have converged in my own life as a Southern Baptist and have had
a part in leading me to make an explicit commitment. Among
those directly related to my relationship and commitment to the
denomination are:

- the call and claim of Jesus Christ for my complete and ultimate commitment to him;
- a study of the kingdom purpose and rich heritage of our
  Baptist people;
- a painful awareness of the vast spiritual need in our world
  for a redemptive visitation from above;

- the need for and process of thoroughgoing denomination renewal that unites and directs lives and energy; and
- a recognition of the spiritual, personal, and sociological forces of commitment in one's life.

Whatever my fellow Baptists do affects me deeply and I care. But as for me, I have had a longstanding commitment to the denomination. During the process of writing this book I have come to articulate that commitment in the following sevenfold statement:

1. I am extremely glad that I am a part of the Southern Baptist denomination.

2. I am committed to the great missionary and evangelistic cause of the people called Southern Baptists.

3. My own personal goals and values as a follower of Christ are essentially in harmony with those of the denomination.

4. I care about the direction, progress, success, and destiny of the denomination and its kingdom work.

5. I am willing to exert a great deal of effort beyond that normally expected in order to help the denomination achieve kingdom ends.

6. I will gladly tell others, within and without, of my loyalty to and support of the denomination.

7. For me this is the best of all possible denominations in which to serve the purposes of God, and it is extremely important for me to remain in this fellowship.

Commitment Toward AD 2000

Commitment to action! Between now and AD 2000 we Southern Baptists are going to be called upon to make many changes. Along with other Americans, we may be confronted with painful decisions as we adjust to what could be a less affluent society.

Our commitment to Christ and his cause will be severely tested. If we see the coming changes as setbacks, thwarting our road to happiness, then disintegration and even despair are sure to set in.

But if we see the shift from an affluent society and a me-first stance as a positive shift, we Southern Baptists could tighten our belts, make sacrificial commitments to responsible choices, make gains in quality of life, and make a significant impact on the total national scene. The following specific areas call for the full range of commitment on our part. *In setting forth this dream, I am not attempting to set goals for the total denomination. But I would dare to give a profile and challenge to the Southern Baptist denomination that is worthy of our commitment to action, together.* It all starts with people and so with population. For our purpose we shall focus only on the population of the United States, although Southern Baptists have a worldwide missionary commitment.

Population Growth Toward 266,000,000

The 1980 census recorded a national population of 226,545,805—up 11.5 percent from 1970. The U.S. Census Bureau estimates that U.S. population will gain 9.7 percent between 1980 and 1990. It will gain another 7.3 percent between 1990 and 2000. (See table in following section.)

In addition to the rate of growth and size of population, Southern Baptists as a denomination of caring and evangelistic churches should seriously consider committing themselves to share their witness with a vast number of people in all age categories. This will involve people of a variety of ethnic backgrounds, languages, regions, localities, and densities of population.

The Bold Mission Thrust commitment to our own nation is to share the gospel with every person so they might have an opportunity to hear the gospel, to believe in Christ, and to fellowship in a local church.

Commitment to Church Membership Growth

Our Southern Baptist people want to reach other people as well as our own sons and daughters for Christ through his churches. A commitment to growth and total church membership is so basic to our reason for being that it should touch absolutely everything we do in the local churches and throughout the denomination. This commitment to growth must be expressed in our priorities and strategies, in the allocation of our resources, in the exercise of leadership, and in how we deal with communication, change, and conflict. Let us consider the following facts:

- One basic standard of Baptist membership growth could be in its relationship to total population growth. "Real growth" is membership growth at a faster rate than general population growth. Real growth indicates a positive level of effectiveness in our outreach and evangelistic efforts.
- Southern Baptist membership has been increasing in total numbers at the rate of almost 1.5 percent annually, as compared to the declining trends among other major denominations. In fact, Southern Baptists have been gaining very slowly in relationship to the growing population in our country.
- During the 1950s, indeed for a thirteen-year period from 1949 to 1962, our church membership grew at an annual rate just over 3 percent, well above the general population growth.
- Commitment to membership growth at a 3 percent annual rate which we experienced during our best years would completely change the picture of our great denomination by AD 2000. This means we would reach approximately 9 percent rather than 6 percent of an increased population. People count! And people reached for Christ in the churches matter! This effort would be worthy of our highest individual and organizational commitment. The following chart should help us get these figures clearly in mind.

Commitment to Increased Resident Membership

Southern Baptists believe in a *regenerate church membership*—a local church made up of baptized believers covenanted together under the lordship of Jesus Christ and

Growth Toward AD 2000

Year	US Population	Southern Baptist Membership	Percentage of U.S. Population
1950	150,697,361	7,079,889	4.7%
1960	179,323,175	9,731,591	5.43%
1970	203,211,921	11,629,880	5.72%
1980	226,545,805	13,606,808	6.0%
1990	248,520,748	17,400,000	7.0%
2000	266,662,762	24,000,000	9.0%

committed to do his work in the world. The increasing numbers of nonresident members and an additional large number of resident members who are inactive in the service of Christ deserve the attention and the caring commitment of churches in our denomination.

- The nonresident portion of total membership has been slowly increasing over the years from 26.2 percent in 1950 to 28.2 percent in 1980.
- The reasons for this increase in non-resident members may be many and must be addressed appropriately. Some causes may be mobile society, membership practices by the churches, methods of evangelism, programs of new membership training, orientation, expectation of congregational involvement, caring environment of the churches, etc.
- A commitment to reverse the trend, practice New Testament evangelism, preach regenerate church membership, nurture the resident members, and build the new membership into the congregation could result in a resident membership of at least 80 percent by AD 2000. This would be more than double the number in 1980.

Commitment to Growth in Number of Churches

In order to reach more people with the gospel of Christ in a more complex and diverse society, we must have an ever-

Growth Toward AD 2000

Year	Total SBC Membership	Resident Membership	Percentage of Total
1950	7,079,889	5,224,958	73.8%
1960	9,731,591	7,061,544	72.6%
1970	11,629,880	8,451,769	72.6%
1980	13,606,808	9,767,343	71.8%
1990	17,500,000	13,125,000	75.0%
2000	24,000,000	19,200,000	80.0%

enlarging number of congregations of every size, shape, and kind.

- We need to commit ourselves to establishing a large number of new congregations in new places, representing a net growth of more than 1.5 percent per year or 14,000 by AD 2000. We have grown by nearly 8,000 in the past thirty years.
- We must commit to the revitalization of thousands of our existing churches to meet the needs of people
  —in the rural areas and countryside;
  —in the urban sprawl and inner city;
  —in the language and ethnic segments of our society; and
  —in the population growth areas and depressed pockets.
- We need to commit ourselves to an increasing number of authentic, Bible-believing, Baptist denominational churches

Growth Toward AD 2000

Year	Number of Churches	Members: Average Size
1950	27,788	255
1960	32,251	302
1970	34,360	338
1980	35,831	380
1990	41,000	425
2000	50,000	480

with a "regional witness" to the masses. Many of these should be multi-language congregations, that are pacesetting in support of worldwide missionary efforts of the total denomination.

Commitment to Sunday School Growth

Historically and practically, our denomination has looked upon the Sunday School as both the Bible-teaching organization of the local church and as its people-reaching organization. We have experienced the fact that "great Sunday Schools build great churches." A commitment to the Sunday School as a Bible-teaching, people-reaching organization is at the heart of denomination renewal. This should be a priority concern not only for local churches but for every agency and institution of the denomination.

Growth Toward AD 2000

	Sunday School Enrollment		Sunday School Attendance	
Year	Number	Percentage of Membership	Weekly Average	Percentage of Enrollment
1950	5,024,553	71.0%	(1967—earliest weekly attendance record)	
1960	7,382,550	75.9%	3,853,568	50.8%
1970	7,290,447	62.7%	3,592,735	49.3%
1980	7,433,405	54.6%	3,792,177	51.0%
1990	10,440,000	60.0%	5,640,000	54.0%
2000	16,800,000	70.0%	10,000,000	60.0%

- First, we must commit ourselves to having a larger number of church members enrolled in Sunday School—from the 54.6 percent in 1980 up to 70 percent by AD 2000. This could be a standard by which to measure our denominational endeavors.
- Within the enrollment of Sunday School, it should be our

intention and effort to enroll a large number of "seekers," those not yet Christians and/or church members who are receiving a gospel witness and a warm invitation.

• We should also be committed to having a larger number of those enrolled actually attending Bible study—up from the present 51 percent in 1980 to 60 percent by AD 2000. The fact that faith comes by hearing and hearing by the word of God is our high motivation for these efforts.

Commitment to Growth in Baptisms

Commitment to evangelism that leads to believer's baptism and discipleship in the local church has everything to do with the purpose and spirit of our Baptist people. Evangelism results are not something we can humanly produce, but we can act faithfully upon the command of our Lord to go and make disciples and to baptize them.

• A commitment to growth will have a direct bearing on the actions we take regarding the number of believers baptized into our churches.

—To be responsible to share the gospel with the total growing population of our nation.

—To be concerned about the total church membership which provides a quantitative way of measuring the performance of the total denominational network of evangelistic outreach.

—To be committed to the enlargement of resident membership as a measurement of the quality of many elements of discipleship in the local churches.

—To increase the number of churches and the spiritual vitality of the churches as "outposts of the kingdom" in a land that is becoming increasingly pagan.

—To enroll a large number of "seekers" in Sunday School for Bible study and friendship.

• Evangelistic results are most often measured by the number of Southern Baptists each year it takes to win and baptize a new convert into the fellowship of our churches. This ratio measurement may not be adequate to fit our theology, the work of the Holy Spirit, the degree of opportunity, or the unbeliever's freedom of choice, but it does provide an objective guage of trends among Baptists.

• An evangelistic commitment on the part of a host of Southern Baptists could move the ratio of baptisms from one baptism for each 31.7 members in 1980 to a more challenging ratio of one baptism to each 24 members by AD 2000.

Growth Toward AD 2000

Year	Number of Baptisms	Ratio of Baptisms to Members
1950	376,085	1 to 18.8
1960	386,469	1 to 25.2
1970	368,863	1 to 31.5
1980	429,742	1 to 31.7
1990	620,000	1 to 29.0
2000	1,000,000	1 to 24.0

Commitment to Growth in Church Training

Commitment to Church Training and Christian development is esssential, not optional, in the forward movement of Southern Baptists. The denominational family has many needs and challenges that can be met only through an effective, comprehensive training program.

• During the last two decades Church Training enrollment has experienced a period of decline from a high of 2.75 million in 1963 to a low of 1.75 million in 1979. More recently a most encouraging turnaround has been taking place. Some have assessed that our reputed loss of identity and rootlessness can be attributed to lack of training.

• Now, we must give our best efforts over a long period of time to such things as:

—Baptist doctrine and beliefs,
—Baptist heritage and polity,
—new membership orientation,
—church membership nurturing,
—witnessing and discipleship training,
—Christian service skills,
—family life concerns, and
—issues and needs in Christian living.

- We must return to a time when at least 25 percent of our total membership is enrolled in Church Training and all that a church family Sunday evening means in the total life of our denomination.

Growth Toward AD 2000

Year	Church Training Enrollment	Percentage of Church Membership
1950	1,440,895	20.4%
1960	2,664,730	27.4%
1970	2,228,217	19.2%
1980	1,795,619	13.2%
1990	3,130,000	18.0%
2000	6,000,000	25.0%

Commitment to Other Church Programs

Church Music enrollment has been increasing steadily in many Baptist churches. Factors relating to this growth trend could be that church music

—is a celebrating element in the worship of our Lord;
—is a part of the total education program of the church;
—expresses the gifts and skills of church members;
—presents an evangelistic, heartwarming appeal to the lost;
—provides an opportunity for volunteerism in missions and service;

—develops an atmosphere of nurturing the fellowship life of the congregation; and

—encourages a commitment to growth as part of the life of the churches and the denomination from 11.2 percent of church membership in 1980 to 16 percent in AD 2000.

Woman's Missionary Union continues to be a driving force in the missions education, missions giving, prayer support, and mission action of the churches among women, young women, girls, and preschool boys.

—WMU has been experiencing changes that could make it a stronger and even more viable organization for an enlarged number of Southern Baptist women to become more fully involved in missions education, prayer and financial support, and mission action.

Growth Toward AD 2000
(Percentage of Total Church Membership)

Year	Church Music Enrollment	WMU Enrollment	Brotherhood Enrollment
1950		1,033,479	167,744
		(14.6%)	(2.4%)
1960	646,698	484,589	619,105
	(6.6%)	(15.3%)	(6.4%)
1970	1,076,487	1,199,813	422,527
	(9.3%)	(10.3%)	(3.6%)
1980	1,527,397	1,100,043	495,666
	(11.2%)	(8.1%)	(3.6%)
1990	2,260,000	1,650,000	780,000
	(13.0%)	(9.5%)	(4.5%)
2000	3,840,000	2,880,000	1,440,000
	(16.0%)	(12.0%)	(6.0%)

—The number of women in the work force and the time available outside the home *and* the work place will continue to place a challenge before this vital organization.

—A growth from 8.1 percent in 1980 to 12 percent in AD 2000 would take a strong, continuous commitment.

Brotherhood enrollment growth among Southern Baptist men and boys would provide a vital link in the total experience of Southern Baptist churches.

—Missions education, prayer support, and mission action can be expanded in order to meet the network of needs and goals.

—Volunteer missionary service is expanding and must continue to do so if Baptists are to reach our nation and the world with the gospel.

—Enrollment growth is challenged from 3.6 percent of the total church membership in 1980 to 6 percent in AD 2000.

Commitment to Christian Stewardship

Giving a powerful, effective witness for Jesus Christ across this nation and around the world will require a commitment to growth in financial stewardship.

- Total for all gifts through the local church for all purposes during 1981-1982 was $2.9 billion, or per capita gifts of $208.57. This represents giving not at the minimum level of the biblical tithe (10 percent) but 1.9 percent of average per capita income.

- Many Southern Baptists are generous, giving far beyond the tithe to the work of the church and Christian causes. Others have not yet caught a vision of eternal investment of their treasures in heaven.

- The success of Bold Mission Thrust and its companion support challenge, Planned Growth in Giving, may lead Southern Baptists to support adequately, even generously, the many different aspects of local church ministry and worldwide witness. Commitment at the point of giving translates into joy for the Christian steward and eternal life for those waiting for the gospel.

- If Southern Baptists by AD 2000 should: (1) grow in numbers to 24 million members, (2) increase in per capita income by an annual average of 4 percent and (3) grow in faithfulness of stewardship giving from 1.9 percent in 1980 to 5 percent in AD 2000, there would be $25 billion in financial resources for doing God's work among the churches and within the denomination. Almost ten times that of 1982! Why should not the people of God think big! We are in absolutely the biggest worldwide business there is—God's business!

Building Toward AD 2000

Year	U.S. Average per Capita Income	SBC Per Capita Giving Percentage of U.S. Average	Dollar Amount
1950	$ 1,506	1.85%	$ 27.86
1960	2,226	2.22%	49.39
1970	3,955	1.86%	73.70
1980	9,490	1.79%	170.14
1990	14,050*	3.0%	420.00
2000	20,800*	5.0%	1,040.00

(*Assume a 4 percent annual increase in US per capita income.)

Year	Total Church Membership	Per Capita Giving	Total Offering Plate Gifts
1950	7,079,889	$ 27.86	$ 197,242,154
1960	9,731,591	49.39	480,608,972
1970	11,629,880	73.70	857,098,689
1980	13,606,808	170.14	2,315,149,038
1990	17,400,000*	420.00	7,308,000,000 (est.)
2000	24,000,000*	1,040.00	25,000,000,000 (est.)

*Projection

Commitment to Mission Giving

The whole purpose of denomination renewal is the authentic experience of a people of God called Southern Baptists fulfilling their purpose, their reason for being. This is most broadly expressed in two dimensions: (1) the local church ministry and (2) the worldwide mission of the churches cooperating together. Commitment by the local churches to mission support has renewing power within it for the total life of the churches.

- Total mission giving for the past thirty years has been at about 17 percent of total offering plate giving. This level of commitment would not support a rapid buildup of the forces for Christ among Southern Baptists.

- A challenging projection is made here for churches to double that level of mission support by AD 2000. That should be possible with increased membership and a deeper commitment on the part of local church members. Conversely, a commitment by the local churches to greater mission support often motivates a higher level of giving by church members.

- Part of the increase in total mission support is needed for local mission projects, support of volunteers in missions, and beginning of new Sunday Schools, missions, and churches. It is also needed for the enlarged support of Baptist associations as they participate in the total growth effort. The state missions offerings and the special home and for-

Commitment to Mission Giving

Year	Offering Plate Gifts	Mission Gifts Percentage of Total	Mission Gifts Amount	Cooperative Program Gifts Percentage of Total	Cooperative Program Gifts Amount
1950	197,242,154	16.9%	33,402,224	0.46%	908,436
1960	480,608,972	17.0%	81,924,906	10.13%	48,689,694
1970	857,098,689	16.2%	138,500,883	9.4%	80,609,946
1980	2,315,149,038	17.3%	401,499,506	8.95%	207,284,435
1990	7,308,000,000	25.0%	1,827,000,000	13.0%	950,000,000
2000	25,000,000,000	35.0%	8,750,000,000	20.0%	5,000,000,000

eign missions offerings will continue to motivate our people
to give.

● In order for the churches to accomplish together a national
and international missions strategy, gifts to the Cooperative
Program will need to double as a percent of offering plate
gifts from 8.9 percent in 1980 to 20 percent in AD 2000.
Every component of the denomination is obligated to the
churches to make such support worthwhile and well
known.

Commitment to Mission Strategy

Gifts through the Cooperative Program support the mission
efforts of the state conventions as well as those of the SBC. The
goal of dividing the Cooperative Program gifts between state
causes and SBC causes has long been that of 50/50, and some state
conventions have made excellent gains in that direction.

● Over the past thirty years, the division of Cooperative Program gifts has been an average of 65/35 between the state
conventions and the Southern Baptist Convention. The state
conventions have the heavy responsibility of supporting new
work areas on smaller resources or larger resources for
both direct missions and institutional effort in the cause of
Christ.

● Accelerated giving by the churches through the Cooperative
Program and a commitment by the state conventions
through the Southern Baptist Convention Cooperative Program would provide adequate funds by AD 2000 to:
—multiply the appointment of career missionaries to the nations of the world to 30,000;
—increase by ten times our home mission forces;
—make a substantial contribution toward providing for the
physical needs of peoples in crisis situations around the
world.
—build an adequate strategy and support system for one
million volunteers in missions annually;

—provide for the theological training of an additional
12,000 ministers of the gospel in every field;
—support a national Christian television network that carries that gospel and the values of Christ into the total
American society;
—support adequately, without government aid or inter-
ference, a strong network of Baptist colleges and univer-
sities that train each new generation to live after the
pattern of Christ;
—provide for the program services and materials needed by
the local churches; and
—start 14,000 new congregations all over this great land of
ours.

Commitment to Strategic Missions

Year	Total Cooperative Program Gifts	CP Gifts For SBC Causes		CP Gifts For State Causes	
		% of Total	Amount	% of Total	Amount
1950	908,436	40.24%	365,596	59.76%	542,840
1960	48,689,694	35.88%	17,470,501	64.12%	31,219,193
1970	80,609,946	34.64%	27,925,301	65.36%	52,684,645
1980	207,284,435	34.62%	71,762,635	65.38%	135,521,800
1990	950,000,000	40.0%	380,000,000	60.0%	570,000,000
2000	5,000,000,000	50.0%	2,500,000,000	50.0%	2,500,000,000

Associations and State Conventions

Guiding and supporting much of our denominational work are
our Baptist associations and state conventions. At the beginning
of 1984, there were 1,214 associations and 37 state conventions.
• Commitment to build toward AD 2000 will greatly depend
on the renewal and vitality of this linkage in the denomination. Significant portions of the new resources given by the
churches to and through these Baptist bodies must be di-
rected toward "new work" and ministries that reach out to-

ward the nation if the commitments listed above are to
become reality.

- If by AD 2000 there is a growth to 24,000,000 members and
50,000 churches, then the number of state conventions and
associations may need to increase by 25 percent. This would
bring the number of state conventions to 42 and the number
of associations to as many as 1,500.

Building Toward AD 2000
Associations and State Conventions

Year	Baptist Associations	Baptist State Conventions
1950	976	22
1960	1,134	29
1970	1,192	29
1980	1,201	34
1990	1,320	39
2000	1,500	42

Yes, the above section is at this time only a visionary profile of
major components of our Baptist denomination. But I am convinced that individual, spiritual, and organizational commitment
must both generate and be fueled by great visionary purposes
among our people. *Commitment to action is the truest expression
of genuine denomination renewal.*

"Are ye able?" still the Master whispers down eternity,
And heroic spirits answer, now, as then in Galilee,
"Lord, we are able," our spirits are Thine,
Remold them, make us like Thee divine:
Thy guiding radiance above us shall be
A beacon to God, to faith and loyalty.

BUILDING TOWARD AD 2000

	1950	1960
	ACTUAL	
U.S. Population (Census Bureau)	150,697,361	179,323,175
Total Church Membership	7,079,889	9,731,591
% of U.S. Population	4.7%	5.4%
Resident Membership	5,224,958	7,061,544
% of Church Membership	73.8%	72.6%
Number of Churches	27,788	32,251
Average Membership Size	302	338
Sunday School Enrollment	5,024,553	7,382,550
% of Church Membership	71.0%	75.9%
Sunday School Attendance	—	3,853,568
% of Sunday School Enrollment	—	50.8%
Number of Baptisms	376,085	386,469
Ratio Baptism: Members	1:18.8	1:25.2
Church Training	1,440,895	2,664,730
% of Church Membership	20.4%	27.4%
Church Music	—	646,696
% of Church Membership	—	6.6%
WMU Enrollment	1,033,479	1,484,589
% of Church Membership	14.6%	15.3%
Brotherhood Enrollment	167,744	619,105
% of Church Membership	2.4%	6.4%
Per Capita Giving (SBC)	$27.86	$49.39
Average per cap. income increase	—	(est.) 4.0%
Giving % of per cap. income (US)	1.8%	2.2%
Total—All Church Gifts—$	197,242,154	480,608,972
Total Mission Giving	33,402,224	81,924,906
% of All Church Gifts	16.9%	17.0%
Cooperative Program Giving	908,436	48,689,694
% of All Church Gifts	0.4%	10.1%
SBC Cooperative Program	365,596	17,470,501
% of Total Cooperative Program Giving	40.2%	35.9%
State Convention Cooperative Program	542,840	31,219,193
% of Total Cooperative Program Giving	59.8%	64.1%
Baptist Associations	976	1,134
State Conventions	22	29

1970	1980	1990	AD 2000
ACTUAL		← BUILDING TOWARD →	
203,211,921	226,545,805	248,520,748	266,662,762
11,629,880 5.7%	13,606,808 6.0%	17,400,000 7.0%	24,000,000 9.0%
8,451,769 72.7%	9,767,343 71.8%	13,125,000 75.0%	19,200,000 80.0%
34,360 380	35,831 425	41,000 480	50,000
7,290,447 62.7%	7,433,405 54.6%	10,440,000 60.0%	16,800,000 70.0%
3,592,735 49.3%	3,792,177 51.0%	5,640,000 54.0%	10,000,000 60.0%
368,863 1:31.5	429,742 1:31.7	620,000 1:28	1,000,000 1:24
2,228,217 19.2%	1,795,619 13.2%	3,130,000 18.0%	6,000,000 25.0%
1,076,487 9.3%	1,527,397 11.2%	2,260,000 13.0%	3,840,000 16.0%
1,199,813 10.3%	1,100,043 8.1%	1,650,000 9.5%	2,880,000 12.0%
422,527 3.6%	495,666 3.6%	780,000 4.5%	1,440,000 6.0%
$73.70 (est.) 6.0% 1.9%	$170.14 (est.) 9.0% 1.8%	$420.00 (proj.) 4.0% 3.0%	$1,040.00 (proj.) 4.0% 5.0%
857,098,689	2,315,149,038	7,308,000,000 4.0%	25,000,000,000 4.0%
138,500,883 16.2%	401,499,506 17.3%	1,827,000,000 25.0%	8,750,000,000 35.0%
80,609,946 9.4%	207,284,435 8.9%	950,000,000 13.0%	5,000,000,000 20.0%
27,925,301 34.6%	71,762,635 34.6%	380,000,000 40.0%	2,500,000,000 50.0%
52,684,645 65.4%	135,521,800 65.4%	570,000,000 60.0%	2,500,000,000 50.0%
1,192	1,201	1,320	1,500
29	34	39	42

Notes

1. Elton Trueblood, *The Company of the Committed* (New York: Harper & Row, Inc., 1961), pp. 10-11.

2. Charles A. Kiesler, *The Psychology of Commitment* (New York: Academic Press, 1971), concepts extracted from throughout the book.

3. Abraham H. Maslow, *Motivation and Personality,* 2nd ed. (New York: Harper & Row, Inc., 1970), pp. 35-58.

4. Daniel Yankelovich, *New Rules* (New York: Random House, 1981), p. 9.

5. Ibid.

6. Ibid., pp. 246-62.

7. Kiesler, pp. 32-33.

8. Kenneth Ferris and Nissim Aranya, "A Comparison of Two Organizational Commitment Scales," *Personnel Psychology,* 36, No. 1 (Spring 1983), pp. 87-98.

9. Thomas J. Peters and Robert H. Waterman, Jr., *In Search of Excellence* (New York: Harper & Row, Inc., 1982), pp. 55-86.

10. Dale D. McConkey, *MBO* for Nonprofit Organizations* (New York: AMACON, 1975), pp. 171-84.

10
Building by
the Blueprints

Challenge #10: As a people of God, let us at all times and under all circumstances, build our lives, our churches, and our denomination on the firm foundation of Jesus Christ and his word.

Matthew 7:24-25: Therefore, everyone who hears these words of Mine, and acts upon them, may be compared to a wise man, who built his house on the rock. And the rain descended, and the floods came, and the winds blew, and burst against that house; and yet it did not fall, for it had been founded upon the rock.

Building on the Rock: In the reconstructed church there must be a basis so strong men can and do hold together in spite of differences. For this of necessity will arise in every church, especially in a church in a democracy where opinions are freely expressed and freely decided upon. This necessity arose in Antioch. . . . The reconstructed church must go over its emphases and its programs and its structures and must eliminate anything comparable to a John Mark issue which is marginal and unimportant and must see that every issue and emphasis in structure and program is central and really Christian—is around Christ.

E. STANLEY JONES[1]

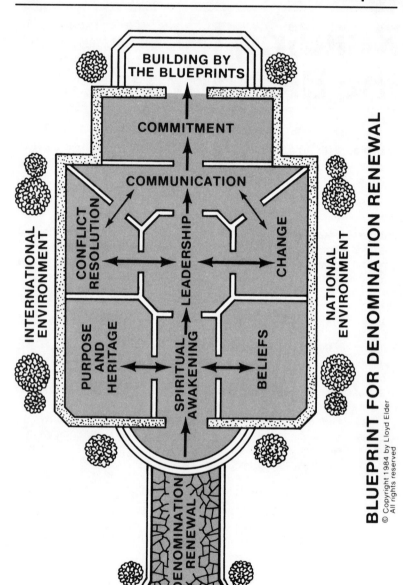

BLUEPRINT FOR DENOMINATION RENEWAL

Denomination renewal! That's what this book is all about. Each chapter, a blueprint in a larger set of prints, has sought to deal with a critical need in our Southern Baptist family. Each chapter has also set forth a practical strategy for genuine renewal.

From chapter 1 in which the appeal for denomination renewal was sounded to the call for commitment in chapter 9, this book has sought to develop a framework for a larger number of Baptists to understand one another better, to face the future with more confidence and hope, and to join their concerted efforts in our high mission. The tenth and last challenge, simply put, is this: *let us at all times and under all circumstances build lives and churches that last, building on the firm foundation of Jesus Christ and his word.*

Southern Baptists are constructing no tower of Babel, no kingdom to rival the place of God among people. Rather, we are engaged in a worldwide mission, one that is worthy of the energetic support of all of us—fourteen million strong. Our cause really matters, here and now, and forever after. We must not miss our place in the purposes and design of God.

Jesus and his word are the blueprints by which we must build. He is the master architect, the pattern for building, the only foundation. Blueprints for renewal among Southern Baptists begin with him and end with him.

This is made quite clear to us throughout the New Testament. One such magnificent text, Matthew 7:24-25, is found at the close of the Sermon on the Mount. In these verses, Jesus set forth at least five truths that give guidance to our building and living. Let us apply these lessons individually and corporately to Southern Baptists in our blueprints for renewal.

We Must Hear Individually the Words of Jesus Christ

"Therefore everyone who hears these words of Mine. . . ."

Southern Baptists are at their best in building lives by hearing the words of Jesus; indeed, hearing the words of Jesus is at the very heart of our mission. Each one of us must hear these words.

"These words of Mine" refer most directly to the teachings of Jesus in the Sermon on the Mount. His words in Matthew 5—7 are to disciples of all times, teaching us about

- blessedness—the way of true happiness;
- salt of the earth and light of the world;
- observing his teachings and personal relationships;
- almsgiving, prayer, and forgiveness;
- fasting, true treasures, and material wealth;
- anxiety and the priority of the kingdom;
- judging others and prayerfulness; and
- the two ways, the two kinds of fruit, and the two foundations.

In building lives today, let us as Southern Baptists remember that the Sermon on the Mount is fundamentally *discipleship teaching*. It has been called:

- the founding document of the Christian kingdom;
- the demands and disciplines of discipleship;
- the pattern and design of life; not an interim ethic;
- a sermon preached, not legislation passed;
- principles to live by, not teachings to restrict us; and
- mandates of the sovereign King, not impossible ideals.

"Therefore everyone who hears. . . ." In a larger sense, this text and others call us to consider the centrality of the total life, ministry, and message of Jesus. Let us also hear the whole biblical revelation that stands before us as God's message of love.

Southern Baptists have a mission to hear individually and to let the whole world hear the words of Jesus. In this text, our Lord urges a universal appeal, "Everyone who hears." We are in the "whosoever" business echoed throughout the New Testament:

- "Come to Me, all who are weary and heavy-laden" (Matt. 11:28).
- "Everyone who calls on the name of the Lord shall be saved" (Acts 2:21).
- "For God so loved the world . . . that whoever believes in Him" (John 3:16).

- "Let the one who wishes take the water of life without cost" (Rev. 22:17).

This *hearing* does not mean just a casual function in daily life. It speaks of an eternal change in the human soul. As the Scripture says, "Faith comes from hearing, and hearing by the word of Christ" (Rom. 10:17). And, "How shall they hear without a preacher" (v. 14) or a teacher, a singer, or a witness?

Our mission is to build lives on Jesus and his word. It starts with hearing. So let us continue to share his word with the saved and the lost, the young and the old, the rich and the poor, the insiders and the outsiders, the lonely and the loveless, our kind and those who are different from us. Let us hear the words of Jesus, individually, universally, urgently, and share them passionately!

We Must Respond Obediently to the Eternal Message

". . . and acts upon them . . ."

That is the crucial difference in the building of life. It is not just hearing the words of Jesus, as important as that is. The foolish man *hears,* but he does not act upon what he hears. Discipleship in the kingdom of Christ demands obedient action.

Jesus clearly and forever impresses on his disciples that obedience is the appropriate response to hearing his word. As Southern Baptists, how shall we respond to that word?

Not arguing the word, but obedience; for there is blessedness in the kingdom.

Not hiding it, but obedience; for we are to be the salt of the earth and light of the world.

Not revising it, but obedience; for there is fullness in the Word of God.

Not merely quoting it, but obedience; for we are to be people of service, giving, and prayer.

Not just adoring the Word, but obedience; for the kingdom of Christ is to have first priority.

Not debating it, but obedience; for we are not to judge others, but all will be judged by the word.

Not refusing it, but obedience; for there is a choice of faith between the two ways, the two kinds of fruit, and the two foundations.

James, the half brother of our Lord, wrote, "But prove yourselves doers of the word, and not merely hearers" (1:22). Also, "Show me your faith without the works, and I will show you my faith by my works" (2:18).

As Southern Baptists, we are at our best in fulfilling our mission by building lives when we not only affirm our complete and total confidence in the Bible as the Word of God, but live out our lives in obedience to its authority.

We Must Build Wisely on Christ, the Solid Rock

". . . may be compared to a wise man, who built his house upon the rock."

We have so much to learn from this text and from our Lord about the mission of building lives. His blueprints are so clear and reasonable. Jesus Christ is not only the eternal Son of God, but he was also the carpenter of Nazareth (Mark 6:3) and a student of Old Testament Scripture.

As the carpenter of Nazareth, he knew the building trade. He knew about foundations and building houses. How many times working out of Joseph's shop did he help build a house? We do not know. In his travels, he must have passed many houses under construction. Did he pause to look at the foundation?

Jesus referred to the wise man who did the painstaking work of cutting into the rock for a solid foundation. Then on this solid foundation he built the structure. On the other hand, the foolish man would simply push back the loose sand on a smooth surface and begin easily and quickly to build. Perhaps the dry sandy place where he built would become a raging waterway during the rainy season.

Encouraging counsel to the Southern Baptist family:

Our world mission program is undoubtedly the most dependable ever developed. We need to support it in ever-increasing giving. We simply must not let the adversary frustrate us now. This can be our finest hour for the glory of Christ.
Carl E. Bates, President, SBC, 1971-1973

Not uniformity but unity in Christ is absolutely fundamental, for it is by unity in Christ "that the world may believe." *What is required is not mere belief that the Bible is authoritative. Of course that is true—even the devils believe that. The essential thing is that we "do the words" of our Lord.*
James A. Langley, Exec. Dir., District of Columbia

Let us make an all-out effort to make Bold Mission Thrust a real priority in every facet of our work from the local church down through the SBC.
Ernest B. Myers, Exec. Dir., Nevada

Southern Baptists have been blessed of God with resources of people and materials. They must all be committed to God without reserve. Then and only then will we see Bold Mission Thrust impact our needy world in the way God intends.
Dan C. Stringer, Exec. Dir., Florida

World evangelization is in God's plan before the return of Christ (Matt. 24:14). Jesus said this gospel shall be preached throughout the whole world, then the end (end of this church age) shall come.
James H. Smith, President, Brotherhood Commission

It is my prayer that we will give ourselves anew to the task of beginning new churches and developing these churches for a worldwide ministry of sharing Christ with every person.
Robert Wilson, Exec. Dir., Michigan

The lesson of Jesus is for us all. The wise man hears the word of Christ and obeys it. He builds his life upon solid rock. The foolish man hears the words of Jesus and does not obey it. His life has no solid foundation.

Being a student of Old Testament Scripture, why did Jesus speak of himself and his word as "the Rock"? The Old Testament believers thought of Jehovah, the covenant God of Israel, as "the Rock." Again and again they testified:

- "The Rock of Israel spoke to me" (2 Sam. 23:3).
- "The Lord is my rock and my fortress" (Ps. 18:2).
- "My rock and my Redeemer" (Ps. 19:14).
- "Lead me to the rock that is higher than I,/For Thou hast been a refuge for me" (Ps. 61:2).
- "God, and the rock of my salvation" (Ps. 89:26).
- "The rock of my refuge" (Ps. 94:22).
- "The shade of a huge rock in a parched land" (Isa. 32:2).
- "Look to the rock from whence you were hewn" (Isa. 51:1).

When this theme is picked up in the New Covenant, Jesus is clearly identified with Jehovah as the Rock.

- "Upon this rock I will build My church" (Matt. 16:18).
- "The stone which the builders rejected,/This became the chief corner stone" (Matt. 21:42).
- "Having been built upon the foundation of the apostles and prophets, Christ Jesus Himself being the corner stone" (Eph. 2:20).
- "For no man can lay a foundation other than the one which is laid, which is Jesus Christ," (1 Cor. 3:11).

What about your own life? I once read the story of the conversation of a successful businessman. He concluded: "All my life I have been building on the things of this world. Now I am building my life on Christ." That is the mission and business of Southern Baptists: to build wisely on Jesus the Solid Rock. All other ground is indeed sinking sand.

We Must Face Realistically Life's Destructive Forces

"And the rain descended, and the floods came, and the winds blew, and burst against that house . . ."

And so it still happens. We do our building against destructive forces all around us. Let us face them squarely and realistically. For us as Southern Baptist believers in the twentieth century, the rain still falls, the floods come, and the winds blow. Personal losses and sorrows belong to the people of God on every hand. (Even as I was working on this manuscript, my ninety-year-old father died, claiming the joy of his heavenly reward but leaving us sad in the journey.)

When it rains, it pours; and the rain does indeed "fall on the just and the unjust." The floods of unbelief, immorality, greed, misused power, and international battle burst against the lives of God's people. The winds of change seem to disrupt and threaten almost everything we hold dear.

What will we do as Southern Baptists in a world turned upside down? Where new religions abound? When our values are rejected? When good families break up? When hard-working people can't use their skills? When new technology drives people into a corner? When communication overload confuses us? When people press for entitlements and rights beyond reason? When we become less and less productive and more and more taxed? When there is a loss of national purpose and a rejection of national and personal humility? When the churches are empty and the stadiums are full? When sin seems to reign supreme in the land?

When it rains, floods, and blows, will we Southern Baptists whine and pout and debate and excuse and defect? No, we will not! As God's people, set in a world to do God's work, we will face this world's destructive forces squarely. We will be obedient to Jesus and his Word. We will build our lives on the Rock. And we will build our mission, our work, and our witness on the Rock!

We Must Live Firmly on the Foundation Rock

". . . yet it did not fall, for it had been founded on the rock."

For those who build life solidly on Jesus and his word, there is a practical and happy benefit. Life does not collapse under the destructive forces. Why? Because Jesus himself is the firm foundation.

Allow me to change the figure from building a house and to illustrate this truth with a contemporary parable growing out of a happy family experience.

In the summer of 1981, our family went to the Southern Baptist Convention in Los Angeles. Following the Convention, we took a vacation to see the magnificent beauty of the western United States. We traveled up the California Ocean Highway to Carmel by the Sea, then crossed to Yosemite National Park, and drove south to the Sequoia Forest to see those giant, ancient trees. We also planned our trip home to visit the massive Hoover Dam on the Colorado River, which I had first seen when I was a seven-year-old boy.

We went to the visitor's center and saw the panoramic model of the Colorado River crossing seven states from the upper Rockies to the Pacific Ocean. We viewed the pictures and films, heard the lectures, and read the brochure. Then we went with a group in an elevator down into that vast structure and out into the power plant.

Hoover Dam, built in Black Canyon between Nevada and Arizona, is one of this country's seven modern civil engineering wonders. Completed in 1935, it required about 4.4 million cubic yards of concrete, poured day and night, seven days a week, for twenty-three months. The dam is 1,244 feet across and 726 feet high. Forty-five feet thick at the crest and 660 feet thick at the base, the dam is built into the solid granite of Black Canyon. The reservoir, Lake Meade, is 110 miles long and 500 feet deep at the dam.

Hoover is an arch-gravity dam, that is, an arch laid over on its side. As I heard this, I realized that the principle of the arch works at Hoover Dam in such a way as to be a parable about the Christian life. The more pressure against the dam, the more it is wedged into the solid rock. I thought about my life and this text from Matthew 7. Oh, that my life were built on Christ in such a way that the more pressure bursting against me, the more my life would be wedged firmly into Christ, the Solid Rock! What a challenge to all of us in the Southern Baptist family!

Hoover Dam was built for three reasons: to control the flood waters of the Colorado River, for water conservation, and for power generation. Again, my thoughts turned to my own life and to this text from Matthew 7. Oh, that my life were built on Jesus Christ in such a way that the destructive flood waters are under his control, that the resources of my life are used for the good of humanity and the glory of God, and that spiritual power is generated to set a light in this dark world! The house, your life and mine, does not fall when it has been founded on the Rock.

Conclusion

The eternal mission of Southern Baptists is building lives that last.

- Let us hear individually the words of Jesus Christ.
- Let us respond obediently to his eternal message.
- Let us build wisely on Christ the Solid Rock.
- Let us face life's destructive forces realistically.
- Let us live firmly on the foundation rock.

That is our mission in the churches and among this great people called Southern Baptists.

Notes

1. E. Stanley Jones, *The Reconstruction of the Church—On What Pattern?* (Nashville: Abingdon Press, 1970), p. 98.

Blueprints: 10 Challenges for a Great People. This book has been a challenge from my life to yours: *As a people of God, let us earnestly seek and together work toward the spiritual and organization renewal of our Southern Baptist denomination.* May God give to us our best days and greatest contribution in service to him. Toward that end I want to lay down my life alongside yours as we build together by *God's* blueprints. Together, as a Southern Baptist family.